MANIPULATE THE DATE

Colin Christopher

MANCHESTER HOUSE
PUBLISHING

MANIPULATE THE DATE

Colin Christopher

Published by
Manchester House Publishing
www.manchesterhousepublishing.com

ISBN: 978-0-9917612-3-4

Credits
Editor: Brenda Robinson
www.potentpen.com

Jacket and Book design by Chris Simon
www.hotspotcreative.ca

MANCHESTER HOUSE
PUBLISHING

Dedication

This book is dedicated to Nadine Harvey and Christine Klein.

Nadine, you were the sister I never had. A common question countless dates have asked me to spark conversation is, "If you could have dinner with anyone, alive or dead, who would it be and why?"

Nadine. I will always have dinner with you. You were taken too soon. I miss you little sister.

Mrs. Klein, I know you preferred your first name, but even now I have trouble calling you Chris. You'll always be Mrs. Klein to me. You were one of the most inspiring teachers I've ever had. You were also taken too soon.

Your Raveen hypnosis records in drama class are where my fascination with hypnosis began. Thank you for playing them. I likely would not be a hypnotist today if you hadn't been my teacher then.

Acknowledgments

To every woman I've ever met, dated, befriended, or been in a relationship with, I'm a better man for having known you. Thank you.

To all the people I've hypnotized, from hypnosis shows to the hypnotherapy chair and everyone in between, you inspire me!

To my friends Anna Manoulik, Anny Slegten, Brian Degenstien, Craig Parker, Darcy King, Derek Perron, Devin LaForce, Gary Quedado, Kori Maleski, Matt Gillott, Morgan Wong, Roger Sharma, Sara McMillan, Sammy Cooray, and Sheldon Fingler, your conversations and wisdom kept me grounded during my hard relationship times. Thank you for being sounding boards and showing me things would get better.

To Rochelle Erricker. Thank you for reminding me there is wonder, beauty, and kindness in the world. Miss you English!

To Bruce Serbin. Thank you for watching the Disney channel with your kids. Who knew it would help lead to this!

And last but not least, to honor a promise, to Megan, Shawn and Dar from the Ramada in Kansas City, thank you for keeping me from walking to the Steak and Shake!

All of the stories in this book are true and based on my personal experiences and/or the experiences of my clients. To protect privacy, all names of people have been changed, and in some instances, small details have been omitted or changed for their protection. That is of course with the exception of Craig in the Introduction. Why not change Craig's name? Well, as you're going to see, I clearly enjoy throwing him under the bus! You're welcome Craig!

Contents

Introduction

It was snowy Christmas night. I had just finished an event where I hypnotized 15 volunteers at a company party inside a community hall, in small town Alberta, Canada.

Craig, my new production manager, was fresh from 7 years working theatres at sea for Celebrity Cruise Lines. We had worked together many times on ships, and he had decided to make the move back home. With his skill and experience, he was a natural choice to coordinate and run my events and I hired him immediately.

It was his first performance on land with me and he did an excellent job! The show was fantastic and there was a lineup of audience members wanting my autograph and to talk to me about hypnosis.

Off to the side of the lineup, one woman stood patiently for about 20 minutes, waiting for everyone to leave. She clearly wanted to talk alone and when everyone in line had left, she walked over to speak. I was expecting her to ask about hypnotherapy regarding a sensitive personal matter that she didn't wish her co-workers to overhear. Craig was a few feet away, within earshot, packing up the last of the sound system.

In a drunken aggressive slur, she asked, "Do you ever just bring someone backstage, rip off their clothes, and take 'em hard from behind?"

I paused. The silence seemed eternal. Suddenly, I heard Craig choke out that cough you hear people make when things get uncomfortably awkward! I angled my body and stared at him: A look of disbelief was on his face.

I crooked my head back to the woman and said, "No…"

Then, as I smiled like an angel, I pointed conspiratorially at Craig and said, "But he does!"

His look of shock was equaled only by her look of disappointment. She turned around and drunk stumbled out of the building.

When she was gone, Craig exclaimed, "That was crazy! Does that kind of thing happen a lot?"

I said, "Oh my God, all the time! Let me tell you about this date I had the other day..."

Over the 2-hour drive home I shared some dating stories and at the end of the trip, Craig said, "You should write a book!"

I thought, "Well, if I do that, it would have to help men and women navigate the dating world and avoid the crazy I've gone through."

There are some very charismatic men and women who get along exceptionally well with everyone they meet; you know the type, the people you feel an immediate attraction to, or connection with. That connection can be in the form of friendship or romance. In some amazing romantic meetings, you might even feel it's love at first sight!

Some men and women are just there. You feel nothing for them and you pass them by.

Then some men and women are difficult to be around and you want to avoid. They're socially awkward and seem to say the wrong thing at the wrong time and irritate you. Sometimes you know why you don't like them. Other times, you can't put your finger on the reasons for your dislike - you just don't feel attracted to them and it's difficult to connect.

When I was younger, especially in the world of romance, I was the socially awkward guy. The outcast. Women did not feel or communicate attraction to me. In social situations, I was always awkward and mostly left out.

For the longest time I thought dating was just luck. I thought my lot in life was to wait for the right woman, and like Hollywood movies led me to believe, one day I'd gaze across a crowded room and there she'd be: The woman of my dreams! I was the nerdy, quiet man, and she would be the beautiful, popular woman. She'd see the potential in me and bring me out of my shell and we'd get married, have babies and live happily ever after.

Hollywood steered me wrong...

In reality, some people have a natural gift - an ability to make friends easily and have wonderful romantic relationships. Others, like me, found themselves socially inept. And so, I had to learn, through research, trial, and error, what comes naturally to some others.

I didn't know this when I first started, but I was in the perfect profession as a clinical hypnotherapist and performing stage hypnotist to learn how charismatic people manipulate others subconsciously - not nefariously, but in a way where they can easily create and participate in excellent relationships.

Hypnosis allowed me to naturally express my fascination with manipulating the subconscious mind to better my hypnotherapy clients and myself.

Part of hypnosis and manipulating the subconscious to be a better person involved studying, experiencing, and consciously practicing human interaction. I voraciously read, practiced, evaluated, and learned all I could so I could consciously Manipulate the Date.

This book chronicles the good and bad of my experimentation, and it dissects, into a learnable process, the subconscious framework that governs dating and relationships.

This subconscious framework not only governs dating and relationships, but also every type of communication and human interaction you participate in, from political elections, to buying a car, to how you perceive your favorite celebrity, or react to a food commercial.

In my experience, charismatic people can naturally navigate this subconscious framework - easily and without conscious awareness of it.

Less charismatic people, like me, can consciously learn this framework and become more charismatic, many times even more so than someone with innate charisma. They can do this because they understand what is happening on a subconscious level and can manipulate that understanding consciously.

The purpose of this book is to outline, explain, and give specific exercises for you to learn and master the subconscious process of navigating this framework, especially focusing on dating and relationships. Once you learn it, you will be able to identify when the subconscious process is affecting you, being used on you, and when you can use it to help yourself.

Learning and properly executing this subconscious process will give you a greater ability to improve your communication skills to create attraction, understanding, and satisfaction between yourself and a potential (or current) mate. No matter your gender or sexual orientation, if you're single, in a relationship, or somewhere in between, you can use and apply the process to boost your confidence and competence in cultivating the meaningful relationships of your deepest dreams and desires.

When it comes to achieving meaningful relationships, there is an insidious lie you constantly hear. In all my years of dating and relationships, my friends and family told me this lie. The media repeats this lie. Hollywood tells you this lie. You hear it so often you can't help but believe it. This lie is told over and over again, especially to children.

To be fair, the lie is well intentioned and meant to help kids develop and have a chance at growing up to be healthy and productive members of society with healthy self-esteem.

I grew up hearing this lie. I heard the lie, or some version of it, often. I constantly repeated it to myself when things went badly in my relationships. I believed the lie for a very long time. The lie is:

You are good enough. You're good enough just the way you are. Inside, you're an amazing person and when someone takes the time and gets to know you, they'll accept you and love you just the way you are.

As an adult, analyzing my failed relationships critically, it was obvious I wasn't good enough to have a successful relationship. After all, if I were good enough, I would have been successful.

If you're good enough to drive a car, you drive it. If you're bad at driving, you crash the car. The evidence of you being good enough is your current relationship status. If you were good enough, you wouldn't be crashing.

If you've been unsuccessful in dating and relationships so far, the objective reality is: You are NOT good enough. But you can be!

That's the really great news – you can become good enough – You can educate yourself, you can change your thinking, you can be a better person.

The catch: You have to want to be better and you have to put in the time, work and effort. If you don't want to put that effort into yourself, that's a clear indicator (ironically) that you're not good enough. Logically, how could you be good enough to invest in someone else if you don't have a burning desire to invest in yourself?

If you truly desire investing in yourself and becoming a better you, you're going to love this book. If you don't wish to invest in yourself, that kind of thinking is the first thing you will have to change. Make the conscious decision to change that thinking right now and commit to investing in the most valuable asset you have: You!

Everyone on this planet has the potential to be a better person. You have to decide to live up to that potential. The good news is you can have much fun becoming good enough to participate in the relationship of your dreams. Yes, there will be time, work, and effort required; but it will be fun along the way. And the payoff will be immense!

As you consciously decide to tap into your potential and you experience the process, some of your emotions will be laid bare and may leave you feeling temporarily hurt or angry: Especially as you recall and resolve bad memories and feelings of hurt. You will also experience excitement, hope and a sense of moving forward towards more meaningful relationships. Stay with the process! And please, when you're experiencing negative emotion, be patient, kind, gentle, and forgiving of yourself.

Become more than you are. Become the incredible person that is the perfect match for the awesome partner you desire. Enjoy and experience the wonderful relationship(s) you want.

Visit me on Facebook, Twitter or my website and share with me how your relationships are progressing.

Facebook: http://www.facebook.com/colinchristopher
Twitter: http://twitter.com/colinontv
Web: http://www.manipulatethedate.com

I wish you luck and great success on your journey!

Colin Christopher
Lake Louise, Alberta, Canada
August 20, 2015

1.
Manipulate the Date -
7 Simple Steps

The process of Manipulating the Date is simple. Like great art, seeing it with your own eyes makes it seem like it takes no effort at all to create. It is so simple it can be broken down into 7 easy steps. Therein lies its beauty. Here are the steps:

1. Planning
2. Practice
3. Interaction
4. Uniqueness
5. Emotional Entanglement
6. Continuation
7. Evaluation

Within the simplicity of these 7 steps rests a multitude of subtle variations. Like great art, context, practice, patience and masterful skill are required to create a masterpiece.

Reading the 7 steps above, they may seem familiar. You are correct. This framework governs the basis of all person-to-person interaction from dating to relationships to sales to political posturing to celebrity endorsements to simple friendships and everything in between. If you have seen these 7 steps before, that's great! You're ahead of the curve. If you haven't, by the end of this book, you will be caught up.

I will discuss and break down the process at length and how it relates to Manipulating the Date and all other person-to-person interactions in coming chapters. For now, regardless of whether you've seen these steps in some fashion before, or they're completely new, you need only see the framework above. This will help you will understand what Manipulate the Date is built on so you can put the process into action.

To begin understanding the subtle variations of Manipulating the Date, let's first see the context and origin of the process.

2.
In the Beginning - The Origin of Manipulation

Like everyone, I grew up a product of my surroundings. My father was an orphan. My mother grew up in post-World War II Germany, and they had nothing. Mom had to take care of her younger brothers and sisters. As a result of the war, both my parents had the classic signs of hardship and abuse that scarred a war-torn generation and went through things as children that no child should ever have to go through.

The result was a couple who immigrated to Canada to start a new life. The challenge with that was they were completely alone, in a country where they didn't speak the language, and with the mentality of growing up in post-war Germany where they had to work 15 hours a day just to have a meal.

They were not very good at social interaction. They fought tooth and nail to eat and survive. Don't get me wrong, I deeply respect their stories of hardship and perseverance, however, because they never had the opportunity to live a normal life as children, they had difficulty raising my brother and me. Money was limited and we grew up in a lower income neighborhood.

My brother fell in with a tougher crowd and was rebellious. He got into a little trouble and they sent him to a boys' school away from home. He was 10 years older than me, and never around when I was little. So each of us grew up somewhat as an only child and our social interaction was limited.

Mom was determined to avoid the issues she faced with my brother. Wanting me to stay out of trouble, she sheltered me constantly. I remember I was around 6 or 7 and got a cavity and because she was distraught about it, she brushed my teeth for weeks on end. She didn't try to teach me how to brush my teeth better; she felt she needed to do it for me. This happened in many areas of my life, but the area it most profoundly affected me was in my relationships with, well, everyone.

Anytime my mother was present she would answer questions for me when people asked me something. The old adage of course, strangers were bad and were never to be spoken to. It wasn't that I was not around other people. I just had no clue how to successfully interact with others because it felt like the opportunities were limited.

I constantly felt insecure, felt I didn't know what to say, and I was worried I would screw up. In fact, I did. At 8 I was playing tag with some kids in the park at school. As I was running, arms flailing as kids' arms sometimes do, my hand accidentally hit the boy beside me in the mouth and knocked out one of his teeth. He was 7 and smaller than me. He bled and cried as a 7-year-old would.

I felt horrible and brought him in to school to the principal's office so they could take care of him. I went back to my class and walked in late. Before I arrived, one of my classmates had told the teacher I deliberately punched the boy in the face and knocked out his permanent adult tooth on purpose. I was yelled and screamed at by the teacher in front of everyone in my class. I watched the clock as she yelled. Five minutes of humiliation and degradation by an authority figure in front of peers I desperately wanted as friends.

Five minutes is the blink of an eye in the grand scheme of life. But to a boy that was already socially awkward, it was an eternity. I spent most of my lunches and recesses alone after that. It didn't matter that it was an accident to anyone in the class.

Mom spoke with the boy's mother that night and it turned out it was a baby tooth that was already loose and falling out. He had a new tooth a few weeks later. But that didn't matter. I was treated like and felt like an outcast. No one wanted to play with me. Thankfully I switched schools the next year. It was always hard for me to make friends, but it felt even harder after that.

The first time I asked a girl out I was fourteen. I had two good friends. Steve and Maria. They were both sort of on the A-List for popularity. They were on the senior volleyball and basketball teams. I wasn't on any of the teams, but we were friends because we used to go to the library at lunch time in the winter and do homework together. Steve was super friendly and always talked to me and included me in conversations.

One day Steve comes up to me at my locker and says, "Colin, Maria likes you! You should ask her out!"

I said, "I like her too. She's great! I'm excited!!! I'd love to go out with her."

But now the pressure was on for me. I had no clue how to ask her out and I was terrified. So I did the smartest thing I could think of and I started avoiding her.

Three weeks went by, with several awkward lunch homework sessions where I barely spoke to Steve or Maria.

One day Steve has enough and pulls me aside after school and barks at me: "Colin, why aren't you asking her out? What's wrong with you?"

I tell him "I can't Steve. I'm too nervous. I've never asked a girl out before. I don't know what to say."

Steve's starts laughing and says, "Is that it? You're gonna do this! It's easy. You already know she likes you, just walk up to her and ask her on a date. Wait for her in the foyer entrance at the beginning of lunch tomorrow, and I'll make sure she walks by you."

Of course, by lunch time, everyone in school seemed to know I was going to ask Maria out. Looking back, I think everyone was excited for it to happen. Steve had put the word out and it seemed everyone knew we liked each other. Students gathered in the lobby to see it happen.

Time slowed down. I looked at the crowd there. Maria walked up to me with a beautiful smile on her face and that look of anticipation a girl gets when she knows the boy she likes is finally going to ask her out.

Time stood still. Sweat dripped down my back. Suddenly I had tunnel vision. Panic! My stomach did backflips! My mouth was dry. When I finally spoke, it didn't feel like I was the one talking. Even to this day, as I write this, I'm not sure what Valentino channeled through me to say the magic words every girl dreams of hearing from a boy:

I said, "So... I heard you want to go out with me?"

Maria took a step back with a look of disgust and replied, "What?" and she stormed away.

The foyer erupted with the laughter of 300 teenagers and it felt like I died inside. There was nowhere to hide. All I could do was stand there and watch. Steve walked up to me and asked, "What the fuck was that Colin?"

I couldn't speak. I turned and walked into the locker room and cried.

Maria waited three weeks for that moment and I screwed it up.

To this day when I bump into people from that school, the "So, I heard you want to go out with me" story comes up.

Maria, if you're reading this, I'm sorry I screwed up. I really did like you.

The humiliation of that day stayed with me for years and I reacted badly and formed a thinking habit where I believed approaching a woman and talking to her would result in humiliation. It took me a long time to get over that self-imposed limitation.

There are many stories I could use to illustrate the multiple factors that kept me from being able to be social. But to sum it all up, the reality is initially I was never shown how, and then circumstances as a child and young adult created a social interaction vacuum in my life. It wasn't my parents' fault. It wasn't my teacher's fault. It wasn't my friend's fault. It wasn't my fault. It was a combination of factors.

Even though it wasn't my fault, it was my life and I had to take responsibility for it so I could function better in social situations. Especially if I ever wanted any hope of participating in a romantic relationship.

Taking responsibility for my social destiny began when I was 25 and working on a cruise ship as part of the entertainment staff. I was at the social center of hundreds of people every day; thousands every week. Constantly surrounded by a sea of people, I had never felt so alone.

As socially awkward as I was, part of my job was to go and strike up conversations with guests. It was actually put into my daily schedule by my boss: "Socialize with guests 4:30 – 5:30 PM."

So, forced to socialize or be fired, I began approaching seniors and speaking to them. To my amazement, people spoke back. My initial conversations were the standard, "Where are you from? What's your name? Tell me about your grandchildren. Tell me about past cruises you were on." And we'd talk.

Mostly I was a questioner and I listened, because I didn't really think I had much to say. But this forced work socialization allowed me to come out of my shell and relate to people and get to know strangers.

I wish I could say my social life thrived after this. It was a little better. I was able to form friendships with my coworkers and speak about things and have conversations. Conversations and interactions were mostly superficial. All that time I still didn't understand how to create meaningful conversations with shipmates or guests on the ship. Conversations certainly happened, but I stumbled into them backwards and almost always felt awkward and out of place. But I was doing it. I was speaking to people.

Now friends of mine, especially from my teens and twenties will most likely say I was very talkative and friendly. But what my friends don't realize is, they were the ones who initiated conversations with me and started our friendship. I'm grateful they did because I was just unable to begin new friendships with anyone without them making the first move. And even then, it took persistence on their part for me to come out of my shell and interact on a meaningful level.

Of course, having friends that were kind enough and social enough to begin friendships with me was wonderful. That is... until it came to starting or having a romantic relationship with a woman.

Imagine a man so socially awkward, a man who could not ask for directions from a bus driver, a man on a cruise ship full of beautiful, eligible women: Imagine a man unable to strike up a conversation! Imagine a man who thought approaching a woman in public, a woman who clearly and genuinely was attracted to him, would result in pure humiliation in front of his peers. Remember my smooth pickup line? "So, I heard you want to go out with me?" Imagine a man, frozen, like a deer in headlights. That was me!

After learning how to chat up seniors about their grandkids in the middle of the ocean, I returned home and made a decision. It was time to meet the woman of my dreams, get married, have some children and live happily ever after.

How was I going to do it? I still could not approach anyone (male or female) under the age of 70 and strike up a conversation. The answer was simple. I had two friends that met their wives on the Internet and I thought, "Well, if they can do it, so can I!"

This is where Manipulating the Date first began.

Step 1: Planning.

It was a simple plan: "The Internet worked for my friends, therefore, I can use it to talk to a woman." It was much easier to sit anonymously behind a computer and send an e-mail than it was for me to talk to someone directly. This substantially reduced my social awkwardness.

To put things into perspective, this was 2002. Internet dating in 2002 was much different than Internet dating today. We were years away from the almighty smartphone with Facebook, Twitter, and the gentle Tinder swipe of left or right. People still felt privacy was more important than posting their drunken party pictures and relationship status on the world wide web.

Internet dating was still very new and it carried a stigma. Many people felt they had failed at the dating game by resorting to a computer to meet someone. I'm probably exaggerating a bit here, but it seemed like half the profiles of women at the time stated, "We'll tell our friends we met at the grocery store" or "Don't tell anyone we met online" or "I can't believe I'm looking for a man on the computer, but here goes..."

And so I put my plan into action and began my foray into striking up conversations with women... Somewhat anonymously behind my computer screen, in the evening, ... I know... romantic, right!?!

Out of that simple plan Step 3 began: Interaction

I can guess what you're thinking: Colin, you forgot "Step 2: Practice." You're absolutely right. At the time, I had no inkling that I could practice how to socially interact with someone. And so, in the beginning, "Step 3: Interaction" came before Step 2.

I sent my first email to Nancy. And I waited. She wrote back!

I was so excited I yelled out, "Holy Shit! This works!"

Nancy and I exchanged a couple emails, and I asked her out. Her picture was beautiful; She was into fitness and working out at the gym

2 hours every day. I was a competitive swimmer when I was younger, and I was exercising a couple hours a day 6 days a week. Fitness and health were important to me, and I felt that commonality was something we could share and build on. Plus, like me, she worked in a facet of the entertainment industry, and I thought, "Hey we've got a lot in common… This is awesome!"

I thought I had met my match! It was Fringe time (a festival that tours the world with multiple theatre productions and street performers) and I planned a walking date ending at the Fringe grounds to watch some street performers.

We met. Well, that's to say, she recognized me from my picture and approached me at the park bench where I was waiting to meet her.

"Hi Colin!" she exclaimed.

I asked, "Hi there, have we met before?"

She replied, "It's me, Nancy!"

It was then that surprising truth became apparent to me:

People on the Internet doctor their pictures.

Nancy, had photo-shopped her picture, was 4 or 5 inches shorter than she said, and easily had 50 pounds on me. Now, although I am attracted to physically fit women, whether you believe it or not, her appearance was not the deal breaker for me. It was the disappointment of her deliberate lies and meeting under false pretenses.

Unsure of what to do in the presence of such a bold face liar, I decided to be nice and continue the date. I started walking with her to the Fringe. A block and a half into the walk we had to take a break as she was becoming winded. We did make it to the Fringe eventually, watched a street performer, and parted ways.

The next day she e-mailed me and asked when she could see me again. I replied that I wasn't interested and she sent an e-mail asking, "This always happens when I meet someone. I like them and they're not interested. Why is that?"

I remember yelling out loud at my computer, "Well, you clearly photo-shopped your picture, you claim to work out 2 hours a day, yet you can't walk a block and a half without needing to rest. You're a fucking liar!" I was angry at being deceived.

But instead of expressing myself honestly I wrote, "It's just me and has nothing to do with you." I didn't have the courage to confront her about it. I regret not being honest with her. Even though she met me under false pretenses, I had felt I should spare her feelings. It was a very immature thought process and attitude on my part.

At the time, I did not understand how to talk to someone in a way that was firm and straightforward while being kind. If I did, I would have been able to communicate effectively with her and still express myself in a way that was true and responsible to my feelings about her deception.

I gained a newfound realization that "people lie on the Internet."

I just reread that sentence and am amazed at my naiveté at the time.

Out of that date "Step 7: Evaluation" was born. Yes, Step 1 to 3 to 7. Slowly I was discovering the framework of Manipulating the Date: Through one new experience at a time.

I thought about what happened, and the clear course of action was: "Talk more online before making a date." This way I would get to know a woman was sincere and could begin a relationship honestly.

And so this is where the structure of manipulating the date began: Based on my experience of that first date. I realized there must be a way to improve my results. Evaluating myself, and my interaction with my date allowed me to create new thoughts and plans that I could plug into the adventure of finding the woman of my dreams.

The second woman I met online, Lana, I spoke with on MSN Messenger. I know, MSN Messenger, such a wonderful relic of the past — how did it ever disappear? Oh right… it kept crashing the computer and was replaced with the reliable, "Any other communication program that was not of Microsoft."

We spoke for two months almost every night for a couple hours. Online our conversation seemed delightful. We exchanged multiple pictures, had fun, flirty banter - I was secretly impressed with my newfound social skill! I learned to banter. "Look at me go!!!" I thought. I had become the king of creating an online relationship. I had met my match and after two months I believed it was time to meet. Lana agreed and we went out for dinner.

We got along very well. She was who she said she was. I was who I said I was. Our online conversations translated exceptionally well into real life. We went out on four or five more dates over the next month, enjoyed each other's company and became intimate. After our night together, we went for breakfast the next morning and somehow got on the topic of her ex-boyfriend.

I asked, "When's the last time you saw him?"

She said, "Yesterday before I came over to your place."

I said inquisitively, "Yesterday? How's that? You came to my place from your house in the morning."

She explained, "Yes, I had breakfast with him."

Dumbfounded, I asked, "How did you have breakfast together at your house?"

She said, "We live together."

Stunned, I said, "You live with your ex-boyfriend? How long have you been living together? When did you break up?"

She said, "We've been living together almost two years and we broke up last week."

I said, "But we've been talking online for 2 months and been seeing each other in person for a month. That's 3 months! You've been with him this whole time and you still live with him?!?"

She said, "Yeah, kinda. We might get back together. I'm not sure. But I like you."

I was pissed: "Yeah kinda?!?!?!?" I kind of never saw her again!

I was dumbfounded that a woman would pursue a relationship with another man while still being in a relationship with someone she lived with. I learned... "Make sure she's single first."

Unfortunately, as you'll see later, that lesson didn't stick with me right away.

It's an easy thing to say, "I would never be with a cheater." In fact, it's easy for anyone to leave a cheater like I did in Lana's case. Although I had developed this relationship over 3 months, I was not in love with her. I only had a weak emotional connection to her so it was easy to break off our "relationship."

It's another thing to leave when you're emotionally entangled. When your emotions are so powerful and so intertwined with another person that it's like trying to untangle a big ball of cat string. It seems like no amount of effort or desire to separate the strands can untangle the chaos.

"Step 5: Emotional Entanglement" was not yet born, but I realized the emotional connection with a woman was part of dating and being in a relationship. That idea began to take root in my subconscious...

From there, I evaluated the Lana experience and my conclusion was:

There MUST BE a better way of Internet dating. The Internet clearly was a way for me to talk with women without triggering the fear I felt from all my social anxiety. The Internet was my panacea to communicate with a woman, just like alcohol was Raj Koothrappali's panacea in the Big Bang Theory. I needed it because of my inability to strike up an initial conversation with someone (other than a senior on a cruise ship!) So I kept at it and developed my system for Internet dating.

"Step 2: Practice" was born! I realized to be successful and weed out the liars and cheaters, I needed to be able to talk to many women and do it in a way that was more efficient than with the two months of talking online to only one woman like Lana.

I decided to begin conversations with more than one woman at a time. Internet monogamy was far too slow. MSN Messenger allowed me to have multiple conversations at once, and because it was written, I could reread whom I said what to, and maintain a proper conversation with multiple women. These multiple conversations were the practice I needed to overcome the lack of dating experience I first had. I developed scripts to start initial contact and created a system based on my observed results. I applied the scientific method I learned obtaining my bachelor of science in molecular genetics – yes, molecular genetics – truly the romance every woman desperately craves!

I received the most responses from women who were new sign ups to dating sites. Through my analysis at the time, I discovered quickly, women mostly checked their e-mails on Monday and Thursday nights. So I'd send out 15-20 emails on Monday and 15-20 on Thursday morning. 30 – 40 in total.

Why 30-40? It was a numbers game. Statistically, of 10 emails sent, three women on average responded. With 30 – 40 emails in a week, I would get nine to twelve responses. From there about 8 women would be open to meet for coffee.

At that point, I would organize a coffee date with women at different locations and times throughout the week.

Coffee shops loved me! There was a cool little spot right by my house that was owner-operated by 2 brothers. They always got excited when I walked in because they loved seeing who I was meeting that day.

Here you would think it was tricky meeting this many women. Except, it was easy. Not because I had become a dating Casanova (I clearly wasn't). It was easy because women on the Internet are notorious for standing men up.

At first I thought it was just me; But after discussions with some of my guy friends participating in Internet dating, they confirmed that like me, women seemed to stand them up about half the time. Many women that showed up to dates with me told me they had also stood up men on Internet dates in the past as well.

In fact, some women felt it was an ego boost for them when they were feeling down. They'd make a date with a man and then stand him up. They enjoyed the attention, and it made them feel better about themselves, regardless of how the man might feel sitting there alone… waiting in hope that she'd show up. The reverse also happens where men stand up women, but it's a little less common. Whether you're male or female, it sucks being stood up.

Think about that for a moment. Let's do the math. Yes, molecular genetics, statistical observation, and math! I know you're asking how I could possibly have been single with all that calculated sexy science?

After perfecting the process to the point of scheduling eight coffee dates a week over the span of five years, I would meet the four women that did not stand me up, I had been on over 1000 coffee dates.

52 weeks X 4 dates X 5 years = 1040
I'm not sure what is harder for me to read in that equation. The five years of being single, or the fact that I met over 1000 women and had no relationship to show for it.

Ok, sure, there were three or four weeks off here and there when I was confident enough to go on a second or third date with a woman and attempt to develop a relationship. At the time, I was bad at relationship development but exceptional at Internet meeting. So when my attempts at relationships failed after a month or two, I went back at it with renewed vigor and made up for lost time.

Usually, on my first week back I'd send out two to three hundred e-mails over the span of that week and organize more dates. My record was 21 coffee dates in 7 days! I had this desire to do three dates a day because it was summer and I felt it was a challenge. Eight women joined me and 13 stood me up.

On a side note, for anyone, man or woman, one of the most disappointing things a person can experience in the dating world is being stood up. If you don't intend to meet someone, don't make the date. Have some respect for others time and feelings, especially when dating. Be emotionally kind.

You may not have an emotional connection, but the other person might, and it's painful when someone is inconsiderate. There's enough relationship pain in the world. When Manipulating the Date, show up and ensure that the person you're meeting feels good about having met you, even if, in the end, you're not interested.

Clearly being stood up is extremely common in the Internet dating world. Unfortunately, it has, or will probably happen to you too. Here is a good practice so you don't feel as bad if it happens: Plan your date near another fun activity that you want to participate in. Then have a 15-minute rule where if someone does not show up, go to your next activity after 15 minutes. I would also always be at least five minutes early so my date didn't have to wait alone and feel uncomfortable. Yes, being five minutes early meant I had to wait for 20 minutes countless times, but having another activity nearby kept my mood positive. If your coffee date is going well, another activity will also allow for a change of scenery that results in the opportunity for you to set yourself apart from most other people who only do a simple meeting on a first date.

This is how "Step 4: Uniqueness" was born. Uniqueness means by comparison to other people your potential partner might meet. Coffee dates can be a very good way to meet someone initially when your only connection is the Internet. But it's not a real date. It's a meeting. For the longest time, I made the mistake of believing a coffee meeting was a real date.

Then, one gorgeous summer day, my coffee date Tanya asked, "Hey, why don't we get out of here and go for a beer on a patio?"

I said, "Yeah, that's a great idea!"

Up until that point, I had never considered going to another place. It's logical and makes complete sense, but I never thought of it. A new location or activity makes it feel like you're on a new date and changes the coffee date into a real first date. I asked my friends whether anyone did this and I asked the women I met on coffee dates if other guys they met ever took them somewhere else after coffee.

Interestingly, based on our collective experiences, coffee meetings without a change of venue or activity rarely resulted in the development of another real date or relationship.

Coffee meetings where places changed were more fun and felt more like a real first date. In these scenarios, a second date was much more likely. Especially, if there was an activity (even a simple walk) involved. Yet almost no one does it! And if they do, like with Tanya, it was by accident.

I attribute this result to an element of uniqueness. As a man participating in online dating, I had to find ways to convey uniqueness to separate myself from the hordes of men assailing women online. And so I did. The two-location date was my first step in this direction. Merely being unique enough from the crowd by separating myself from the competition and having a two-location meeting/date was enough to substantially increase the likelihood of having more dates with someone I liked. Plus, when I did it right, it was more fun! And if I was stood up, at least I got to do something more fulfilling than sulking back home disappointed and alone.

More experience, more evaluation, and adjustment of my plans and dating practice ensued. The biggest benefit of practice; It helped me get over much of my social anxiety and allowed me to refine my initial interaction with women. It also allowed me to meet women that were less likely to stand me up.

I was able to rely on women coming to meet me much more regularly when I learned how to start conversations and convey my uniqueness in a way that separated me from other men online. This uniqueness fostered the continuation of communication with women into full-fledged dates.

"Step 6: Continuation" was born. Through my evaluation I realized to develop a relationship from dating, it's not enough to only go for coffee. You had to have ways of continuing the relationship from planning activities and having the freedom to ensure communication persists.

I refined the process testing many e-mails and the final result of my years of experimentation to have the greatest success at starting conversations and meeting for a date on the Internet was this:

Hi, I'm Colin.

I really like what you had to say about yourself and I'd like to get to know you better.

I'm sure you're getting contacted by all kinds of men with no manners and/or brains, but if you're looking for a man with both, read my profile and write me back.

Colin

That was the best way to begin a conversation with an intelligent woman. I pointed out the two obvious perceived shortcomings of the men contacting them (no manners and/or brains). Women prefer men that treat them with respect and dignity and can hold a conversation – and the same goes for men. Unfortunately, there's not a lot of that going around on the Internet. How do I know this? One question I always asked my dates: "Tell me the craziest story of a man hitting on you online."

They always proceed to tell me guys send them nude/dick pictures, or ask them to fuck, or they send them insulting e-mails when they don't respond favorably to them.

The way women are treated online is despicable. As a man, treating a woman with respect and being a gentleman sets you apart. I shouldn't have to say this, but it is pathetic that in this day and age, men still think they can be an asshole to women and wonder why they're single. Now when I say gentleman, you can have tattoos and look like a biker and still be a gentleman. Women like men of all physical descriptions and vice versa. This has nothing to do with looks, it has to do with your demeanor to women and people in general.

So, after starting the conversation by pointing out the shortcomings of other men online, the result (almost always) was the woman I contacted read my profile.

This is where I portrayed even more uniqueness. Keep in mind, everything I wrote about myself is true. I always recommend the truth. It's the best way to begin any relationship. It is how the truth was presented, in a fun and interesting way for the reader, which made the profile successful. Again I tested many profiles, but this was my most successful one that lead to dates, especially when I used it in combination with that first e-mail above:

I'm into enjoying my life. I have fun. I've been skydiving, scuba diving, downhill skiing, and the most dangerous activity of all, walking across a dance floor where the bride was throwing the bouquet to the single ladies...let's just say I got a few high heels where high heels are not meant to go...ok not really, but I have caught the garter at a wedding and danced with the girl who caught the bouquet at the request of the bride and groom... she wasn't my type seeing as she was 12...

But yes... I can dance.

I like beautiful things, and from time to time I like to get my hands dirty with things like renovating my house...yes I have a house...and all my hair...pretty good, eh!

Yes, I say eh from time to time... I am Canadian!

I like to joke... I like to laugh... I'm always smiling.

I exercise frequently, weight lifting, running, swimming, yoga and you should like physical activity too. I give big bonus points if you do yoga or at the very least you would come with me to class from time to time.

Are you a woman that's independent...? You know what you want... You pursue what you want... You have a healthy lifestyle... You are intelligent... You are thoughtful... You do what you love... You are single... You are at peace with yourself...

You are thinking... I really want to meet this man.

Here I am. Come meet me.

Colin

The key elements of uniqueness that set me apart from other guys and worked were good grammar and spelling, showing I had responsibilities in my life I took care of, showing I was fun, and it showed women an idea of the kinds of activities we could participate in together if we were in a relationship. It sparked their imagination and conveyed my personality to them while in the back of their mind they were comparing me to men with no manners or brains. This created the perfect way to ask for a date immediately with very little time spent talking online. Meeting in person is almost always different than meeting online and I recommend always continuing the process and meeting as soon as possible. Then continuing with fun activities and more dates.

Whether you like it or not, or agree with my method, the process worked. The steps of Planning, Practice, Interaction, Uniqueness, Continuation and Evaluation were realized.

In fact, the process worked so well, it allowed me to meet her: The woman that changed my life. The woman that brought me more joy than I ever thought possible and allowed me to express myself and become an emotionally mature man. The woman that laid me bare and destroyed me. Destroyed me mentally, emotionally and spiritually.

I have never loved anyone more.

I have never hated anyone more.

Elaina.

3.
The Foundation of Emotional Entanglement

My relationship with Elaina began with occasional e-mails and then long talks on MSN Messenger. She was hyper-intelligent and I could tell she was used to shutting men down and not giving them the time of day because they weren't her intellectual equal. Neither was I. But I had a great deal to offer – a higher value than the average Joe on the Internet. As a hypnotist, my career and experience were unique and separated me from the rest of her suitors. I think that's why she agreed to meet me.

As I spoke with her online, I conveyed my uniqueness while combing conversation with our common interests in science and worldviews. Her responses to my questions were refreshingly unique and our banter went far beyond the usual lame conversations of, "Hey what are you up to this weekend?" and "What kind of car do you drive?"

I was drawn to her intelligence immediately.

On our first coffee date at Starbucks, she was very late. Almost 30 minutes. I don't know why I stayed past 15 minutes. As I said earlier, I had established a 15-minute rule long before. I often wonder what would have happened if I had obeyed the 15-minute rule and left. So much destruction in my life would have been avoided if I had followed that rule. But then, so much love would have been lost. I'll never know what the better road would have been.

Our coffee date created an unusual emotional bond. Normally emotional bonds in relationships occur through sharing experiences, especially those that are out of the ordinary or exciting. If you think of one of your best friends, you can always identify and remember the emotional experiences that have created your closeness. Usually, experiences that create emotional bonding are positive, but this can occur in stressful situations too, like a patient in the hospital befriending a caregiver.

Our unusual emotional bonding occurred as we were discussing my life working on cruise ships. It's a fascinating topic, filled with excellent stories of my travels to exotic locations through the Mediterranean, South America, the Caribbean and Alaska.

As I spoke about my travels, she became interested in the psychological aspects of me being moved from ship to ship every couple of months. I explained that I managed to settle in and begin forming friendships and then I'd have to leave for another ship never to see my new friends again. It was a rollercoaster of emotions and a painful time for me.

Earlier in this book I spoke about how my friendships only formed when others approached and spoke to me first, and being the new guy shipboard, friendships didn't happen right away anywhere I went. Then people would start friendships with me only for me to lose them. I didn't tell her about my shyness. I only told her I made and lost friends on a constant basis and it was mentally and emotionally draining and left me very lonely and heartsick.

She asked me, "Were you ever in a relationship onboard?"

I said, "Yes, but it ended badly. She decided to be with another man instead of me."

It was a lie draped in a veil of truth. In fact, I had developed a deep friendship with a woman that I grew to love very much on one of my ships. We talked every day, had meals together, and worked together. We shared deep conversation and it was an amazing time in my life. I told her how I felt, but she was not interested. Shortly after I told her, I left the ship and she began dating someone else. I never heard from her again. It very much felt like a breakup to me.

So the story was close enough to the truth of me being in a relationship that it didn't feel like a lie. Still, the memory of all the pain and loss I went through was revealed and I shed a couple tears in front of Elaina. I felt them roll down my cheek. I felt vulnerable in front of a woman I deeply respected.

Later in our relationship I remember having a conversation with Elaina about our first date and she said, "That's when I knew I had you. I liked you the first time I met you, but when you cried, I knew you were mine."

Step 5: Emotional Entanglement was born. To have a successful date and relationship, there has to be an emotional connection to start. This connection must be developed to a point of entanglement. At the point of entanglement, relationships become cemented together. Emotional involvement can be created many ways: Sharing your deepest hopes and fears, sharing experiences (good and bad), etc. The key is they must be shared. You can't become emotionally entangled with each other if only one person is experiencing an emotional relationship. This is key when manipulating the date and beginning a relationship. Both people experiencing and sharing emotions together are what create the continuation of the process. Without sharing, "Step 6: Continuation," stops and the process falls apart.

From the moment I shed my tears, our relationship flourished. We spoke on the phone for two to three hours a day, and when we were in the same city, we'd spend as much time together as our schedules allowed.

I shut down my Internet dating accounts and focused on developing our relationship. Although I had been in relationships with other women for short periods of time, this was truly the first time I had considered changing my life and creating the space to get married.

I placed my trust in her, shared my hopes and desires. She shared hers and we became emotionally entangled. Our relationship felt amazing. That was until she got sick.

At the time, she was working in a different city. We were on the telephone and she was having massive pain and collapsed. She managed to get a neighbor to take her to the hospital, and she told me she had ovarian cysts and was pregnant. I dropped everything and raced to see her and spend time with her.

During our time together when she was first sick, she said two other men were pursuing her and visiting her. I was devastated that she encouraged these men to see her instead of telling them she was with me. She aborted our baby girl, and we broke up. It was the end of November and we spent Christmas apart.

We spoke one day just after Christmas and talked about how we missed each other. She told me she was just going out with those 2 men to make me jealous and nothing had happened with either of them. I chose to believe her and we got back together.

But she was lying to me. She was developing a relationship with one of those men. There were signs I ignored, believing I could trust her. But one day in March we were out for breakfast and Murray called. She went outside the restaurant claiming it was a work call, and she'd be right back. What she didn't realize is we were sitting beside an open window, and I could hear her conversation. It was clear she was in a relationship with him and attempting to hide it from me.

I confronted her about the phone call. She continued to claim it was work. I lost it. All semblance of calm left me. How I screamed and yelled. I'm still ashamed how out of control my emotions became.

About a month later she called me up and informed me she was single and sorry. She told me she wasn't really sick with ovarian cysts. She actually had cancer and didn't tell me. She said she didn't want to put the burden on me all those months back and she was only dating Murray to take her mind off of the cancer and she really wanted to be with me and she broke up with him.

Mentally I was confused. Emotionally I was hurt. I told her I needed some time to think. I needed to sort out my feelings and so I went traveling for three weeks. During my time away I decided to forgive her and came to the realization that I wanted to be with her and create a life together. I justified her cheating behavior as a part of being sick and I thought she deserved another chance.

I arrived back home and called her to set up a date and talk in person about getting back together. Her cell phone was disconnected. I called her work and they said she no longer worked there and had moved. Having no other way to contact her, I knew she was at a conference in a neighboring city the coming weekend. She had invited me to it before I left so I drove to see her.

There I saw her holding hands with Murray, talking to people at the conference. I was stunned. She had lied to me again. She apparently had not broken up with him.

I approached them both and handed her a gift I had chosen while traveling that I thought would help us reconnect. Murray was obviously pissed that I was there. I don't blame him. We were both being lied to. I was a ball of contempt and rage myself. I wanted to beat the shit out of him. But I managed to keep my cool and walked away.

The next day she showed up at my door. We spoke for hours. I told her I wanted to be with her and she said she wanted to be with me. She said it was over with Murray and would break it off. I believed her.

I believed her until I saw the announcement of their engagement on Facebook by Murray's sister a few weeks later. His sister had tagged Elaina at their family dinner showing off the engagement ring.

At this point, you're probably asking how I could keep putting myself through this. Elaina was clearly a liar and toying with my emotions. And you're right. She was. But my emotional entanglement blinded me to her lies. My emotional entanglement created my desire to believe she was better than she was. I was in love and emotionally adrift in a sea of lies and half-truths and was too immature to untangle myself. I was a slave to irrational thought. I ignored the truth. I ignored the cheating. I felt powerless against the onslaught of my emotions.

In fact, it wasn't until she got married that I finally realized how destructive she was to me. A few days before she married she showed up at my house and told me it was over with her and Murray and she wanted to be with me again. I told her to clean up the mess she was in with their families and calling off their wedding. I told her when things were resolved we could talk about where we would go from there and I would be with her. She agreed. I was still emotionally entangled.

But something was wrong. I didn't hear from her for a few weeks so I did a quick Internet search to see what I could find. And that's when I saw them:

Their wedding pictures!

She married Murray… The man she cheated on me with and left me for.

Words can't express the feelings of pain and betrayal I felt. It was as though she had raped my soul. She had duped me with the lie that their wedding was called off and used me to cheat on Murray days before their wedding.

Depression set in. I stopped exercising and gained 50 pounds. Parts of my beard turned grey. Business took a dive. I started having heart problems. It felt like everything in my life was failing. I had fallen apart and I had no motivation to do anything. I saw myself as the victim of a woman who rejected my heart, soul, and all the most intimate pieces of me that I shared with her.

In retrospect, despite how I felt, I was lucky. I no longer had to put up with her lies and cheating. That was now Murray's domain. Despite being married, Elaina still wishes to cheat on Murray. Although they moved and now live in a different city, and notwithstanding the fact that I've blocked Elaina's phone numbers and e-mail addresses, she calls me from restricted numbers and randomly shows up at my house when she's in town. She's looking to cheat on her husband. She always claims things are going badly and they're getting divorced. Of course, she's lying. But emotional entanglement no longer blinded me to the truth. Yes, my emotions still affected me, but I could now make better decisions because of the circumstances.

She's unhappy with Murray but won't leave him. I've asked her why countless times. She says, "If I leave him I'm afraid I'll be alone. You won't be with me anymore. What else have I got?"

I feel sorry for her when she shows up at my door. Despite my empathy, finally, I was able to stop letting her in.

The Colin I have described in this book up to this point: The socially awkward, emotionally immature, serial dater was dead. Inside and out.

It was time for a new beginning.

4.
The Evolution of Manipulation

I wish I could say that it was like a light turned on in my brain and I turned my life around on a dime.

It wasn't like that. Not even close. It took four years of Elaina and Murray being married to stop letting her into my headspace. Although Elaina was married, as I mentioned, that did not stop her from wanting to cheat. As I said, even with phone numbers and e-mail accounts blocked, over those four years Elaina erratically showed up at my house every month or so. It was brutal on my mental and emotional health to have her turn up randomly. In the beginning, I attempted to be civil and be a friend. But when she arrived at my house, she was there to cheat on Murray.

I almost always became furious at her lies and we fought. It felt impossible for me to heal the wounds that our relationship and our arguments inflicted upon me. As I said, I was depressed, overweight, health failing, and my business was struggling. Many times, it felt like all I had left was our fights.

It was easy for me to give relationship advice to clients in my hypnotherapy practice, but it seemed impossible for me to follow my own advice and the advice of my friends and cut the cord when it came to Elaina. My argument was always, "Well she shows up at my house randomly. I have no control over her."

It didn't help that Murray suspected her of cheating and had contacted me on several occasions by letter, email, and phone, threatening me. I kept the documents and recordings of the voicemails for police records just in case. But thankfully, he was all talk and no action. The problem in their marriage wasn't me. The problem was they had a bad marriage and he blamed me for it. Elaina did too. Apparently my not wanting to talk to either of them and blocking them meant I was interfering with their happiness somehow and they both seemed to want me to suffer for it. From their perspective, the foundation of lies they had built their relationship on was clearly not the problem...

I spoke to two lawyers about restraining orders and tried obtaining a peace bond against her to keep her from showing up at my house. But the justice of the peace all but laughed at me saying, "You're in no physical danger from her. You're a man and she's a woman. Get over it."

Sage advice.

He was right. I was in no physical danger. I was only in mental and emotional distress and I guess that doesn't count. The cycle continued... After three or four weeks, I'd start to feel better and then she'd show up at my house. Each time, my reaction to her pushed me back into my deep dark hole of depression. A vicious circle of pain I could not escape.

For a long time, I contemplated the reasoning behind that. I clearly could not control her actions, but my reactions should have been under my control. I had deep emotions that clouded my judgment and thought process. I knew the answer was within me, but I could not find it.

And so, after four years, I finally had enough sense to take a different approach: I searched outside myself and examined the relationship problems my hypnotherapy clients were having. I analyzed the entire hypnotherapy process they were going through.

I was able to help them resolve their relationship issues, and yet somewhere, as I was going through the therapy process myself, it was breaking down. I participated in psychology sessions, had hypnotherapy sessions and listened to a lot of Wayne Dyer speech recordings. Something about the way Wayne spoke was soothing and kept me from doing anything drastically stupid and harmful to myself. Thank you, Wayne. I would love to have met you to thank you in person, but as I write this, a few weeks ago you passed away. Rest in peace Wayne. And thank you again.

I wasn't achieving any measurable results in improving my mental and emotional health. And so I thought, "Ok. Let's pick the modality I'm most familiar with: Hypnotherapy. If I deconstruct the process down completely into its components and then analyze my situation bit by bit, I think I can narrow in on where it is I'm failing myself."

In my analysis, I observed hypnotherapy sessions follow a basic pattern:

1. **Planning** – The client makes an appointment and I instruct them to take specific actions. For example, download and listen to my free relaxation MP3 online so they can become familiar with hypnosis before the session (If you're interested in the free relaxation MP3 visit http://www.hypnosishealthstore.com and sign up to download a copy).
2. **Practice** – The client follows the plan and listens to the MP3 so they are ready to be hypnotized by me personally.
3. **Interaction** – We start with an intake interview where the client(s) discusses their goals for the session.
4. **Uniqueness** – The session is custom tailored to the client based on the information discussed in the intake interview and on their objectives.
5. **Emotional Entanglement** – Various hypnosis techniques are used to emotionally intensify the goals of the client as well as resolve past emotional entanglements so the client is no longer triggered by the circumstances that create their reactions.
6. **Continuation** – With the session complete, an additional phone consultation is scheduled for follow-up.
7. **Evaluation** – The client observes their reactions over a period of time and reports on the results during the follow-up and the process is repeated if and where necessary based on the experience and evaluation.

I looked at that hypnotherapy pattern for a long time. Mulled it over in my mind. I knew it worked when I applied it to other people. So why wasn't it working on me? The answer still eluded me.

A few months went by and the answer came from another area of focus in my life. Being a self-employed entertainer and speaker, I had to learn early on how to sell myself. As part of that process, I'm always looking for ways to be better at sales and I took a highly specialized course that delved specifically into the mind of high profile buyers. Because of my depression at the time, my business was failing and it seemed like a perfect way to get back on my feet and take my mind off of the distress I felt.

The sales process they taught was complicated. It seemed like a lot of: When the buyer says A, respond with B to get result C and with C do D, E and F so the client will do X, Y, Z, etc. Because of the confusing complexity I thought, "Ok, there must be a simpler way of doing this." And so I analyzed my notes and what I learned in the course and broke it down into its basic components:

1. **Planning** – Research the buyer.
2. **Practice** – Role-play scenarios and be prepared for the sale.
3. **Interaction** – Contact the buyer.
4. **Uniqueness** – Ask probing questions to discover their particular set of problems. Most sales people offer a solution without knowing the true problem of the client. Discovering their issues sets you apart from these other salespeople.
5. **Emotional Entanglement** – Discover, through questioning, how the problem makes them feel. Offer a solution to their problem that will alleviate the emotional dilemma they are in.
6. **Continuation** – Book the speaking/training event and/or schedule a time to offer a greater in-depth solution if they need more information.
7. **Evaluation** – Make notes on the interaction and identify areas that can be improved and implement more planning.

I thought, "This looks really familiar. Where have I seen it before?" Then I saw it. The pattern of the sales process was the same as the pattern of a hypnotherapy session. So I naturally thought, I wonder if this applies to my Internet dating? And for the first time I wrote it out. I knew the process subconsciously. I had never summarized in on paper before.

1. **Planning** – Decide on the dating website I want to use to make a date.
2. **Practice** – Write out a profile.
3. **Interaction** – Send e-mails and make a date.
4. **Uniqueness** – Show them what makes me different from other men.
5. **Emotional Entanglement** – Ask questions that create topics of conversation that are emotional (preferably positive) and participate in activities that elicit shared emotional excitement.
6. **Continuation** – Make another date.
7. **Evaluation** – Think about how it all went and what can be improved on next time and make a plan to repeat the right parts of the process.

I had my 7-step process for manipulating the date distilled down to its core elements.

In researching my first book, Success Through Manipulation, I came across an interesting book called The Game by Neil Strauss. The book is about Neil becoming one of the greatest pick-up artists in the world, and his book is a fun and fascinating read. When you read the book and look at the chapter titles (written below in steps 2 to 6), you can see the pick-up artist process follows the same structure.

1. **Planning** – Reading the book, learning the process and setting yourself up as a pickup artist.
2. **Practice** – Memorizing routines.
3. **Interaction** – Select a target, approach and open.
4. **Uniqueness** – Demonstrate value, disarming the obstacles, and isolate the target.
5. **Emotional Entanglement** – Create an emotional connection
6. **Continuation** – Extract to a seduction location, pump buying temperature, make a physical connection, blast last-minute resistance, manage expectations.
7. **Evaluation** – Journal the experience and debrief with other pick-up artists and see where you can do better next time.

Seeing this process duplicated in multiple areas gave me a fresh perspective on the hypnotherapy steps I was putting myself through and I finally saw the issues with my thinking around Elaina and myself.

I spent a great deal of time focusing my efforts on resolving my mental anguish and emotional problems with Elaina, but as I evaluated the results I kept missing one critical factor. I was focused on Elaina and the relationship and the lies and the betrayal. At no point was I focused on me and becoming a better person.

In my evaluations and discussions, I kept including how I thought about Elaina in the process and it kept me from healing. This wasn't her fault; It was mine. By failing to take her out of the evaluation and new planning, my situation with her kept repeating itself. Despite her severe shortcomings, when it came to treating me with any honesty, commitment, or relationship respect, I kept letting her back in.

I wasn't altering how I thought about myself. I was constantly thinking about her, her betrayal, and her lies. Those continuous thoughts plugged themselves back into the process and created more and more subconscious emotional entanglement: Angry, bitter, and depressing despair.

I saw the steps applied everywhere, and then applied it to my situation. I plugged my own thought process in to resolve the issues I was having with letting go of Elaina. I couldn't keep her from showing up and attempting to cause chaos in my life, but I could manipulate my own thought process using the pattern I had identified in multiple disciplines on myself.

And so began the evolution of thought that gave rise to the process I'm about to lay out for you. Before I could be ready to let go of Elaina and participate in the loving relationship I wanted; before I could Manipulate the Date with another person, I had to Manipulate the Date on myself.

I focused on myself. I focused on being a better person. I focused on having a better relationship with myself. Before you begin dating and relationships with other people, I encourage you to examine your relationship with yourself. This way you'll become the better person that is ready to have a healthy relationship with someone amazing.

5.
Manipulation of Self -
The 4 Pillars

Manipulation of self begins with developing the ability to evaluate oneself objectively. To do this, you must have self-awareness and be able to set aside your emotions and ego. This skill can be difficult because you will be taking a very long hard look at your successes and failures to see where you need to improve. When things are going wrong, it's easy to see your circumstances and other people's and justify things by saying, "I did this because someone else did that! It's not my fault."

That kind of thinking won't get you far. The questions you will pose to yourself will be based on taking responsibility and asking yourself: "What did I do to contribute to this result? And, what can I do to create a different and better outcome?"

To be successful, you must develop the skills to be objective and take responsibility. You are the master of your fate in the dating world and in every area of your life. If you take the time now to develop these skills, not only dating but every area of your life will benefit!

Of course, Manipulate the Date began with a plan. And this time I had the process. I decided there were four principal pillars of self-health that had to be mastered:

1. **Physical health**
2. **Mental health**

3. **Emotional health**
4. **Spiritual health**

For me, this is the order that the pillars should be worked on. The reason is as you go through the process, each builds upon the last making each pillar easier to manipulate.

The easiest pillar to start working on is the physical because you have immediate access to it and it's simpler to focus inwards and work on the mental, emotional, and spiritual when your physical health is good. For example, right now, you can start with eating a proper meal and going for a 15-minute walk. By comparison, can you really tackle psychological issues as quickly as going for a walk? Likely not.

As you go through this book, some components will be more important to you than others. Work on them in the order that feels right to you. Do what makes the most sense and seems best. But take the path of least resistance and work on the most natural pillars first so you have small wins that build on each other to build your momentum. Without momentum, tackling harder emotional challenges can seem overwhelming.

Most people have chosen this book because they are having dating and relationship issues and are looking for help with that. You have the opportunity to date and have relationships and friendships with almost anyone, however, as you develop and mature the relationship with yourself, your other relationships will improve because you can give the best of yourself.

After all, when you're developing any relationship, you likely want the best from the person you are pursuing. If you want the best from them, you owe them the best from you. Ensuring your health in all areas will give you the greatest opportunity to be successful as you go forward and pursue successful relationships.

If you are getting over the end of a relationship and getting ready to move on, here are some guidelines to help you get back to being healthy as fast as possible:

1. Exercise: It reduces stress and releases hormones that alleviate depression.

2. Eat healthy: This keeps your body from getting run down. It's easy to become an "emotional eater" or "emotional starver" when you've gone through a breakup. Focus on being an "emotional healther" when it comes to food.

3. Avoid drugs and alcohol: They're depressants and, in the long run, keep you down when you already feel bad.

4. Get out of the house and be around happy, fun people: Emotions are contagious. Surround yourself with positive ones to lessen the pain of the negative ones you're feeling. Participate in fun activities you really enjoy. It could be mountain climbing, exercising, bird watching, taking that trip to an exotic locale with your best friend or whatever. Do whatever you have to do so you feel better.

5. Stay away from Bridget Jones Diaries, The Notebook and other Hollywood romance movies and romance novels: These set unrealistic expectations of what a good relationship is supposed to be, especially when you compare them to how your past relationship just ended.

6. Stop looking up your ex on Facebook, Twitter, Instagram and other social media: Knowing he/she is having fun and living life without you can compound your pain. Don't have any more contact with each other. When you're fresh out of a relationship, there is a tendency for the person who was dumped to reread old emails, love letters, and even try to 'accidentally' have a run in with their ex. One of the best ways to move on is to forget about them altogether. Delete old emails, take them out of your contacts list/phone book and don't spy on them.

7. Stay away from video games: These keep you isolated. Get out and socialize with friends.

8. Change your thinking: If you are constantly reliving and thinking

about the negative aspects of your past relationship(s), it takes its toll by contributing to low self-esteem and decreased confidence. To combat this, spend at least 10 minutes every day reciting positive thoughts or affirmations. For example: "I am strong, confident, attractive and make a great life partner."

9. Take a break: Give yourself as much time as you need to recover. Don't let anyone pressure you into believing you have to jump back into dating or see other people immediately. Emotional healing is not a race and only you will know when you're ready.

10. Seek support: There is no reason to ride the emotional roller coaster alone. Talk to close friends, family members, or a therapist you feel comfortable with. Find a local support group and talk to others who are going through the same thing.

11. Don't play the blame game: Whether you feel the breakup was a result of your ex-partner's actions or something you did, stop playing the blame game. See it as a learning experience and put the focus on moving on.

12. Stay away from all of your other old exes: When you go through a breakup, that feeling of being wanted and needed is missing. It's not easy conquering your feelings of loneliness. It's tempting to contact a long lost ex who knows you well and could make you feel comfortable and wanted. While this might seem like a good idea, it can hold you back from moving on because you won't be resolving your current relationship issues or helping the future.

13. Focus on the future: When you're ready to move on, think about what your life will look like next year at this time. Where you are, what you're doing, what kind of people are in your life, etc. This will give you hope and a sense of purpose.

14. Forgive yourself: Being hard on yourself manipulates you into feeling despair. Forgiving yourself creates feelings of hope for the future and eventually feelings of gratitude and happiness. Those positive feelings are far more attractive to new potential partners than negative ones.

15. Allow yourself to mourn the future relationship you thought you would be part of: You're not just mourning the loss of what was and is, but also the relationship that could have been. All the potentials that you saw for your future will never be fulfilled with that person. Much of the pain you feel is not from missing the past relationship, but the future one you thought was to happen.

6.
The First Pillar -
Manipulation of the Physical

Manipulation of the physical is the easiest pillar to improve yourself simply because you have direct access to your body. You can change locations, you can change your diet, you can move more or move less, etc.

For me, being 50 pounds overweight with heart palpitation issues, I clearly had to get my health back on track. With the go-ahead from my doctor, I talked to one of my best friends and we arranged a workout routine. Monday, Wednesday, Friday. 5:30 AM. 60 – 90 minutes of intense weight training. It took 8 months and my heart finally began beating calmly, regularly and properly. 12 months later I lost the fat and finally felt physically healthy… for the first time in years. Now I did say, the physical is the easiest to manipulate, but depending on your physical conditions and abilities, the results do take time. It's not always a fast process depending on your goals.

I was a competitive swimmer when I was younger. I felt like I needed to get back into that shape so that my body wouldn't die on me. But my long years of absence from the gym and becoming not very fit caused physical pain when exercising the likes of which I had never experienced before. The pain was brutal to overcome. In fact, after every workout I was so tired and sore I didn't think I could do it. I had to sleep 2 to 3 hours after a workout because I didn't have the energy to stay awake no matter how early I went to bed. Then I would get up and I could not bend over far enough to tie my shoes without an overwhelming feeling of pressure in my chest. It felt like it was about to explode.

This is how I felt physically EVERY day for eight months. Slowly I lost some of the fat, my endurance levels returned to a normal level and my body could recover from the physical soreness. Then one day, eight months later, I bent over to tie my shoes and I was pain free. I yelled triumphantly, "Fuck yeah! It doesn't hurt!" I had forgotten the simple pleasure of pain-free movement, and the feeling was incredible.

But to get through that rough period of physical pain, I used the process. I don't know your health situation, but I do know there are always physical challenges to gaining, regaining, and maintaining health and fitness. But the end result is worth it and you can do it! That is if you're emotionally entangled with your plan. I'm going to tell you how I went through the 7 step process and then I will lay out the key questions you will ask yourself to make the decisions to help you manipulate and master the pillar of health.

1. Planning - Being a competitive swimmer the planning part was easy for me. I made the decision to exercise and get healthy no matter what, and to help me; I added being accountable to a workout partner, Jerry, to keep me going, no matter the circumstances. Then I chose a workout routine. Once I was in the gym the combination of accountability and routine kept me from having to think about the process. I could focus on execution and just do it: No matter what.

2. Practice. – With the plan in place, I visualized what the workout would feel like and thought about how I would feel after completing my first workout. Throughout the 12 months, I spent 5 minutes or less visualizing before about two-thirds of my workouts.

3. Interaction – Here, there were two conversations that I always had: The first was the conversation with myself and the second was my conversation with Jerry. I told myself, "I can do this." In fact, I say that to myself before every exercise. The conversations with Jerry just happened naturally.

4. Uniqueness – There was no uniqueness with the physical workout.

The uniqueness came with the conversations I had with Jerry. We've been friends for years, went to high school and university together, and we both have degrees in molecular genetics and so we both have interesting topics to speak about. This broke up the monotony of the physical workouts and kept my mind engaged and distracted from the repetitive exercises.

5. Emotional Entanglement – Being excited about exercising and regaining health was a big problem for me. As I said, for the first eight months I was in constant pain throughout my entire body. Although I told myself, "I can do this," at every workout, when I finished I told myself I don't know how I can go on.

Emotional motivation took place on multiple fronts for me. The first was the fear of my heart failing. Fear is a powerful motivator in the short term, but a terrible emotion to become entangled with in the long run. Never the less, for eight months it was a primary driving factor in my exercise. But once my physical health felt like it was back under my control, that fear was gone. Relief and excitement replaced fear, and that came from experiencing a wellness in my body I had not felt since before meeting Elaina. I finally felt a light at the end of a very long dark time in my life.

The other emotional motivation was my conversations with Jerry (I call him Jerry after Jerry Seinfeld because he's funny). We tried to be light and joke around. We both have a favorite Simpsons episode where Homer gets ripped lifting weights at the gym with a German movie action hero named Rainier Wolfcastle. So, like Wolfcastle motivating Homer, we "Shout Powerful Motivational Slogans" at each other in cheesy German accents. We're always joking around. Keeping an upbeat attitude allowed me to mentally look forward to the workouts even though I dreaded the physical pain I would subject myself to.

The final emotional motivation was that if I didn't show up, I would be letting Jerry down. At the time, letting myself down wasn't a big deal, but the guilt of letting someone else down emotionally motivated me to the idea of showing up. Like the fear motivation I just spoke about before, guilt is a terrible long-term motivator, but for eight months it was another motivator to get over the physical pain and show up at the gym. Once the pain was gone, the guilt also disappeared to be replaced with excitement for the energy I enjoyed from being healthy again.

All of these emotional motivators together have emotionally entangled me with exercise and allowed me to overcome the pain for those first eight months.

6. Continuation – Each workout Jerry and I agreed to talk or text the night before to ensure the other would be there the next morning.

7. Evaluation – Every workout I constantly thought about how I felt and what I could change or augment to exercise more effectively. As the first few workouts progressed, I had doubts in my mind. When it came to lifting weights, with each exercise I did, I was only able to lift a half to a third of what my body could have done only four years before. I was stunned at the amount of muscle strength I had lost. I had no idea how much my body had deteriorated, and it was a rude awakening.

Right from the start I had to adjust the workout plan to accommodate the demoralization I felt at losing that much strength and the overwhelming physical pain I constantly felt. Over the span of the 12 months it took me to get completely back in shape, my workout plan was altered based on this evaluation. I changed weight lifting programs four times to alleviate injuries sustained and to exercise smarter and better.

That is the summary of my process. Now let's look at it for you. Answer the following questions for each of the seven parts of the thought process behind physical interaction with yourself. Regardless, whether you are a competitive athlete, a couch potato, or somewhere in between, whatever your health and physical conditioning, I encourage you to go through this process. To make things easier, you can get a copy of these questions and all the rest of the questions in the book including space to write in a downloadable PDF file at

http://www.manipulatethedate.com

1. Planning

1. List your top five health goals for the next six months. If you're an athlete, list your top five performance goals. For example: Reduce stress, have a healthier diet, lower blood pressure, curl 50 pounds with 1 arm, be able to walk 10 flights of stairs without breathing hard. Or as an athlete – win a specific event or increase muscle mass by one or two pounds, etc. The list can be as general or specific as you need it to be while focusing not on activities, but specific results you desire. Once listed, number them from 1 to 5 in the order of "ease of achievability," from 1 (easiest) to 5 (hardest).

2. For each goal, list one or two actions that you can take that will move you closer to the objective. Start with the easiest and give yourself an easy action you know you can complete. For example, if one of your goals is to eat healthier, an action could be to eat a salad every day or to drink water instead of soda. If you want to curl 50 pounds with one arm, then maybe it's come up with a routine to get you from where you are to where you want to be in six months.

3. For each of these goal and action scenarios, list obstacles that keep you from taking action and achieving your goal. For example, if you are overweight, an obstacle you may face is being too heavy to walk for a long enough time without hurting your knees. Or you may find there are no obstacles, but usually there are, otherwise you'd already be taking the action. Maybe your obstacle is a lack of will power.

4. For each goal/action/obstacle scenario above, list a solution that you can implement. For example, if you are overweight and have difficulty walking, a solution might be going to a doctor or personal trainer and getting professional advice on a diet to lose weight and get to the point where it is easier to walk and/or eventually run. If you're an athlete, maybe an obstacle to winning your next event is the distraction of a negative teammate. A solution may be to sit down and talk to them privately, or avoiding them completely to keep you mentally focused on winning.

5. For each goal/action/obstacle/solution scenario above, describe how it feels to fail at each goal and then describe how it feels to succeed at

each goal. Start with the words: If I fail to…. I will feel…. Finish with the words: If I succeed in… I will feel…

You are not allowed to use the words, bad, sad, happy or good. You must be more descriptive. If you need to use a thesaurus, do it. The more descriptive and discerning you can be about your feelings here, the more successful the process will be for you in the long run.

For example:

If I fail to lower my blood pressure, I will feel paralyzing remorse and feel like I have let my family and myself down.

If I succeed in lowering my blood pressure, I will feel ten years younger and have amazing energy and excitement about the future of my health!

On a side note, if one of your goals is losing weight, there is a free hypnosis for weight loss resource to help you at:

http://www.freeloseweighthypnosis.com

2. Practice

Although your health is a physical goal, you must be mentally prepared to achieve the physical. And so, begin by practicing mentally. Call it what you want: Mental review, visualization, self-talk, prayer. Think of it as mental preparation for success. Begin with the easiest to achieve result you chose and work backwards. See yourself implementing the solution you came up with that allows you to overcome the obstacle(s) that keep you from taking action. Imagine how you feel overcoming that obstacle. Next, see yourself taking the action(s) that bring you closer to achieving the result you desire. Imagine how you feel taking that action. Finally, see yourself achieving the result you desire and imagining how that feels.

For example: If your goal is to eat a salad instead of a triple cheeseburger and fries, take a minute and visualize what's standing in your way. Maybe it's lack of willpower. So see yourself with strong will power. Imagine how great it feels to have that willpower. Next see yourself getting the salad at your next meal. Imagine yourself enjoying the salad. If that's a stretch for you, imagine yourself excited and surprised that you made the right choice of eating that salad. Imagine how good it feels to achieve your goal.

With this mental rehearsal, you've set yourself up for success, and when you physically do it, you'll feel even better about achieving what you practiced in your mind. This is because you will have created a double win (one mental win, and one real world win), and that double win develops momentum to help you overcome the obstacles you wrote about in the planning stage. Winning also creates an emotional motivation that leads to the emotional entanglement that is coming up.

3. Interaction

Now it's time to put your mental practice into action. Go back to your planning work and begin with the easiest to achieve result you chose, take action, and observe your results — pay attention to positive or negative results, and pay particular attention to how you feel.

Once you've done the first, go through the rest and once again take note of your results and feelings.

4. Uniqueness

In going through the manipulation process for personal physical results, some people find it difficult to create uniqueness to break up the monotony and time required to see and achieve measurable results. Especially when going through the first round of this process.

Now that you've mentally and physically achieved what you practiced and took action on, take some time and list one or two things that you can incorporate or combine with each of your actions to make the physical process unique and achievable for you. I.E., what sets the activities apart for you this time versus before you plugged yourself into this process?

For example, the uniqueness of my workouts was provided by conversations with my workout partner. For dieting, researching and trying new recipes that are exciting and healthy vs. the standard plain salad helped me. Instead of walking on a treadmill for 15 minutes you can walk outside and look for new stores and visit a new part of town. Maybe you listen to audio books on topics of interest while bike riding.

Many times, the key to creating uniqueness for achieving your physical goals is by engaging yourself mentally. What can you do mentally that will allow you to achieve the physical?

5. Emotional Entanglement

You will notice in planning, practice and interaction, you have been learning, imagining and observing how you feel. Your feelings and how they intertwine with the physical results you desire will be the deciding factor in your success.

Examine how you have felt in achieving the actions that are bringing you closer to the results you desire and compare them with question 5 (If I fail/If I succeed question) in the planning section. Decide if your feelings have changed or if they've stayed the same now that you've gone through the process for the first time.

List anything(s) you can do to increase your excitement and/or fall in love with the goal/action/obstacle/solution/feeling scenarios you're participating in to achieve your physical results.

6. Continuation

Set two dates and times where you will participate in the next round of your goal/action/obstacle/solution/feeling scenario. The first date and time will be for the next step (Evaluation) and then planning and practice. The second date and time will be to begin your next interaction where you follow through with your planning and practice.

When working on improving the physical pillar of health, there are two steps in this process where people usually fail. The first is not following through on continuation. Failing to schedule a time for evaluation, new planning, practice and/or failing to schedule a time for the next interaction will stop your momentum and leave you stuck. If you don't schedule the time now, life, family, friends, and work will conspire against you to ensure your failure. Set your times. It's ok to set the time for evaluation, planning and practice ten or fifteen minutes before you start taking action(s) and as you gain experience, and become competent, you may find you only need three to five minutes to complete these steps.

Also, if you've gone through the planning and practice but not yet taken action, schedule a time for your first interaction phase right now. It's understandable that if one of your action steps is going to the gym and it's the middle of the night, you can't do it right now. But you can schedule when you're going to do it.

The second step where people usually fail is they never get past the planning stage. The thought process is usually: "Read everything first and start later." The problem is they never go back and begin the process. If you just read through all the questions and do not take the time to write anything down and really participate in the process, you probably won't come back to do it.

Take the time, go back, and do it now. If you don't have the time to go through the process now, then do the continuation and schedule a time when you will go through the process and do it then. You'll thank yourself later.

7. Evaluation

Now it's time to go over everything you've done and consider your results by asking yourself the following.

1. What are the unexpected challenges you faced by taking action to achieve your results? List them. For example: If you are exercising more, is there physical pain that is difficult to overcome? If you are dieting, are you having trouble controlling your appetite? If you have a medical

condition, are there side effects that are holding you back?

2. Regarding these unexpected challenges, what can you do to overcome them? Who can you get help from to overcome them? How can you adjust your plans to be more successful?

3. Was there anything that surprised you about going through the process? What was it? Can you use this surprise to adjust your plans and be more successful?

4. In your planning, practice, and interaction with your goals, are there any results you want to add? Are there any results (now that you've tried obtaining them) that you want to remove?

5. Is the pursuit of your goals adding or taking away from your general wellbeing? Are they improving your relationship with yourself? Are they improving your relationships with others?

6. Are the results you desire truly contributing to your pillar of physical health? Or are they actually a detriment?

7. Compare your results with your planning and practice. Does your plan need adjusting? Does your practice need adjusting? Does your interaction need adjusting? Does your uniqueness need to be more enticing for you to stay motivated? Does your emotional entanglement need to be stronger? What can you do to make your emotions stronger when it comes to your plan?

8. It's common knowledge that substance abuse like excessive alcohol and smoking will shorten your lifespan and cause a host of health issues. Are there substances that you are abusing? Is it time to reduce or eliminate these substances from your lifestyle to increase your health? If so, what can you do to achieve this?

9. In all of this, are you being honest with yourself?

10. Are you pleased and delighted with your results so far? If not, what

can you change in your plan to ensure you are happy?

11. Is there anything else you feel you should ask yourself and find the answer for, to ensure your success and physical health? If there is ask yourself the question(s) and discover your answers.

Based on your answers to these questions, review and adjust your plan accordingly.

7.
The Second Pillar -
Manipulation of the Mental

An estimated 18.5% of Americans over age 18 had a mental illness in 2013, according to the report, "National Survey on Drug Use and Health: Mental Health Findings," by the U.S. Department of Health and Safety Services. That's 43.8 Million people. If you take that percentage and apply it to the rest of the planet, that's well over one billion people who suffered some kind of mental illness in 2013. According to The World Health Organization, 350 million people suffer from depression worldwide. There are other statistics with varying percentages depending on the study and the year. No matter the hard stats, it's safe to say that either you, or someone you know, could be, or has been affected by a mental illness at some point.

Things are happening around the world and in our own backyards: War, terrorist attacks, school shootings, random street fights, and arguments at home. Highly emotional events can trigger mental illness. There is help. To be very clear, this book is not a substitute for professional help if you require it. If you feel depressed or have any other issue, seek the help of a professional therapist that you feel is appropriate. If you're not sure what you need, it's your right as a human being to get help. Go see a medical doctor and they will refer you to someone that can help, I encourage you to do so.

I was depressed for an extended period of time after my breakup with Elaina. At first I couldn't sleep. When I did sleep, I could only get about 1-2 hours a night. I was sleep deprived because I could not calm my mind down long enough to rest properly. I lost my appetite and lost 25 pounds and stopped exercising.

After 3 months of this, I was so exhausted mentally and physically I slept 12 to 15 hours a day. My appetite returned and, over time, I then put on 50 pounds.

Certainly, there were times when work required me to have regular sleep hours, but for the most part over a 4-year period, I slept the afternoons away. I had little to no energy. My mind constantly thought of Elaina and how devastated I was that she left me for Murray. It felt like I was in a deep dark pit of despair I couldn't get out of.

I had never experienced this kind of continued lack of hope and lack of desire to take action in my life. It was very scary.

I don't know where you are in your life. I hope as you read this you are healthy mentally. If not, depending on your condition, as I said earlier, I encourage you to seek professional help. What follows are many of the questions I asked myself to help me determine what type of help I needed. My answers allowed me to objectively identify where I needed help and what some of my problems were. It also allowed me to get help.

Some people view mental health issues as a weakness. They're not. If you fell and broke your leg, you would go to the doctor and get help for your leg to heal. The same applies to your mind. For me, all I needed was the right combination of professionals and my own desire to get mentally healthy to receive the push I needed in the right direction.

1. Do you feel you need to escape emotional situations and/or daily life through the use of drugs, alcohol or other means such as smoking, excessive sleeping or adrenaline rush activities, etc.?

2. Do you skip meals, binge eat, or overeat because of emotional turmoil?

3. Are you on any medications that have possible side effects that may alter your mental outlook?

4. Over the last six months, have you felt lonely? How often? Does this loneliness affect your mood, relationships, day to day life, and/or your work in a negative way?

5. How many close friends do you have? List them. Do you feel enough support from them to feel safe talking to any of them about how you feel mentally and emotionally?

6. During the last six months, have you ever been so worried about something that you could not sleep at night? How many nights? Is this a recurring issue or has it resolved itself?

7. During the last six months, have you ever seriously thought about suicide? Have you sought professional help?

8. Do you constantly feel tired? Do you have very low energy or difficulty focusing?

9. Over the past month, have you missed work, school, or other daily activities you regularly participate in because of feelings of hopelessness or other emotional distress?

10. Do you find yourself engaging in adventurous activities that endanger your physical health or your life? These activities include sexual intercourse with multiple partners without proper protection and placing yourself in harm's way in traffic.

11. Have you been involved in a traumatic event(s), such as a mugging, sexual assault, physical attack, stressful military actions, discovering a deceased person or pet, the death of a loved one, or an emotional fight with a family member or friend? If so, does thinking about the event cause you stress? Does this stress lessen over time, or is it constant, or does it increase? Are you able to function typically in day to day life in the presence of this stress or does it hinder you?

12. Do you hurt yourself, on purpose, physically on a repeated basis? Or,

do you repeatedly put yourself in emotional situations that cause you pain, such as getting back together with a cheating ex, only to see them cheat on you over and over?

13. Do you feel that you are a victim of circumstances on a constant basis where one person, multiple people, or everyone is conspiring against you?

14. Are you bullied at school, at work, or other situations on a constant basis? If so, how does it make you feel? Are you able to stand up for yourself or do you feel you need help?

15. On a scale of 1 to 7, how happy do you feel about your life in general? 7 is extremely happy and 1 is not happy at all.

16. Have you suffered any physical or health trauma, such as a broken limb, chronic injury, cancer, organ removal (such as kidney, gall bladder, etc.) that is causing you mental or emotional distress?

17. On a scale of 1 to 7, how healthy do you feel? 7 being extremely healthy and 1 being not healthy at all.

18. Do you find it difficult to make decisions that used to be very easy or find day to day life is harder to cope with?

19. Is there anything else you feel you should ask yourself to preliminarily assess your success and mental health? If there is ask yourself the question(s) and discover your answers.

Based on your responses to these questions, decide if you should seek the advice of a doctor, mental health professional, a friend or family member or someone else. If you're not sure, talk to your doctor and find the help you need and deserve as a human being. Sometimes, all you might need is a good talk with a friend who will listen. Get yourself mentally healthy.

I'm asked why I put the physical pillar of health before mental health. The answer is simple. Exercise improves mood and releases hormones in your body that lower stress. There are many studies on this that you can easily reference on the Internet. Just exercising on a repeated basis alleviates mild and moderate depression and can help with severe depression as well.

Depression certainly is not the only mental illness people suffer from, but it's very common, especially when people are getting over breakups and wanting to create a new relationship. It's also one I personally experienced. Working on the physical pillar of health first helped condition me to climb out of my pit of despair.

8.
The Third Pillar -
Manipulation of the Emotional

Emotions!

They start, stop and turn on a dime. In a microsecond, a woman in labor can be screaming at her husband, "Never touch me again!" and then the doctor places her newborn baby girl gently in her arms and she experiences divine love.

You can watch a horror movie where you laugh as the comic relief says a funny joke and then look on in horror, seconds later, as the monster gets him!

You can feel the icy cold grip of anger clench your heart and pierce your soul as the person you love leaves you.

You can feel the exciting rush of anticipation, excitement, and ecstasy when you kiss the love of your life.

You can laugh so hard you cry. You can cry so hard you laugh.

Emotion. Let's ride that roller coaster!

In business, making emotional decisions is usually costly and logical analysis is generally profitable. Why? Because emotions can cloud judgment. However, emotion also drives top performers. The most successful performers have a fire inside that drives them to greatness.

But the question is, "How do you harness the power of your emotions while making logical decisions to experience the best of both? Especially when it comes to dating and relationships?"

When I hypnotize clients in hypnotherapy sessions, emotional manipulation is the primary factor in success. Resolving negative emotions that keep a person stuck in bad habits that create poor results is the key to allowing them to make sound and logical decisions free of the influence of their negative emotions.

When I looked at my relationship with Elaina, I was afraid of losing her to another man. I felt I wasn't good enough to be with her and this fear clouded my judgment. When she left, fear was replaced by the devastation of having my fear realized and the loss of the life we had together. I desperately wanted that relationship back; and so when she came back, there was always a little hope that she would be with me forever. I felt the life I lost with her could be resumed. That small hope was keeping me from healing. Hope is a powerful emotional driver. Ironically, hope was also what was keeping me down and depressed: It emotionally clouded my judgment and kept me from making the logical decision to move on and start over with someone new. I had to stop hoping: And so I killed hope to regain happiness.

1. Planning – My plan began with a decision that no matter how I felt, no matter how much it hurt, Elaina's influence would be removed from my reality. I could not control her entering my life when she randomly showed up at my house, but I could eliminate the reminders of her in my life when she wasn't there. I made a plan to purge all reminders of her – pictures, gifts and clothing she left at my house.

2. Practice – At first I had no idea how to implement my plan. I couldn't imagine what my life would be like without her, so instead I imagined what my life was like before her. In general, before I met her, I was in a good mood most of the time and I was a happy man. So I visualized the memory of feeling happy and being in a good mood.

3. Interaction – I had no idea how to start the conversation with myself to remove the influence of the pain I felt thinking about Elaina. The practice of visualizing myself feeling happy and in a good mood did not make me feel better, especially in the beginning, but it did keep me focused on finding anything that did make me feel better. Instead of sleeping my afternoons away on the couch, I started conversations of emotional wellbeing with myself by turning on the Comedy Channel. I watched anything that would make me laugh. I forced positive emotions down my throat until I felt like I was in a better mood.

In the beginning, the improvements in my feelings were temporary, but when I felt better for a few minutes I would take something that reminded me of Elaina and throw it out. It took me a couple weeks to find everything that triggered my emotions about her and got rid of them. I wanted to get rid of everything all at once, but it was too painful for me to do that, so I spread it out, bit by bit.

4. Uniqueness – Exercising, watching comedy, and purging belongings were not unique however these three things combined slowly shifted my emotional state away from depression. I began to feel like a human being again and that was a uniqueness I had not felt in a long time. This uniqueness provided the motivation I needed to continue to take steps to feel better and remove the emotional influence I was allowing into my life by thinking about Elaina.

5. Emotional Entanglement – As I slowly began feeling like a human being again, my self-worth began to return. I hated letting go of the life I had envisioned for Elaina and myself. I was in love with the potential of that life. But the positive feelings of my self-worth returning, laughing at funny jokes, and relief at not thinking of Elaina constantly allowed the hope I had felt for us to die. As that hope died, I became entangled with the feelings of a new hope, hope for the new possibility of a better relationship with someone who was faithful and wonderful.

6. Continuation – I made the commitment to myself on a daily basis to watch comedy on TV so I'd feel better.

7. Evaluation – As I felt better I found new ways of improving my mood. I sought the help of a psychologist and another hypnotherapist to dissect and resolve my emotional issues. I committed to spending time with friends and family when I could and I focused on doing things that improved my mood wherever possible. As I did this, I actively sought out conversations and activities with people that replaced the influence of my thoughts and feelings about Elaina.

That is the summary of the emotional process that worked for me. Now let's look at it for you by answering the following questions for each of the 7 parts of the thought process behind emotional interaction with yourself. Regardless of your emotional health, I encourage you to go through this process. Again, if you want a copy of all the questions in the book, including space to write, you can download them in a PDF file at:

http://www.manipulatethedate.com

1. Planning

1. Describe the situation in your life that is currently bringing you the most emotional satisfaction. This can be related to relationships, dating, work, family, self-esteem, etc.

2. Describe the advantages of this current emotional satisfaction.

3. Describe what you appreciate most about your emotional satisfaction.

4. Describe the situation in your life that is currently causing you the most emotional distress. Describe the emotions you feel regarding this situation. This can be related to relationships, dating, work, family, self-esteem, etc.

5. Describe the disadvantages of this emotional distress. What do you feel this distress is keeping you from experiencing?

6. Describe what you resent the most about this emotional distress.

7. Describe how you would like this situation in your life to be if the distress, disadvantages and resentment were resolved, and you felt emotional fulfillment. Describe the emotions you would like to feel. If you're having trouble look at your answers to the first three questions to see what emotional fulfillment looks like in another area of your life.

8. Reread your answer to question 7 and describe one or two (or more) actions that you can take that will move you closer to your emotional fulfillment. Start with the easiest and give yourself an easy action you know you can complete. For example, if letting go of the angry feelings you have towards an ex will help you feel better, an action could be to write out the qualities in a partner that make you feel good. Another action might be to sit down with a friend or a therapist to talk about your feelings and get them off your chest.

9. For each of these emotional fulfillment/action scenarios, list obstacles that keep you from taking action that moves you closer to emotional fulfillment. For example, if you have trouble letting go of your ex, maybe an obstacle is you're ashamed or embarrassed to talk to a friend about the situation. Or you may find there are no obstacles, but there usually are, otherwise you'd already be taking the action.

10. For each emotional fulfillment/action/obstacle scenario above, list a solution that you can implement. For example, if you are embarrassed to talk to a friend, then looking for a friend that is supportive and nonjudgmental may be helpful, or talking to a professional may be the right option. You can find a solution that works for you.

11. For each emotional fulfillment/action/obstacle/solution scenario above, describe how it feels to fail reaching emotional fulfillment and then describe how it feels to succeed. Start with the words: If I fail to.... I will feel.... Finish with the words, "If I succeed in... I will feel..."

You are not allowed to use the words, bad, sad, happy or good. You must be descriptive. If you need to use a thesaurus, do it. The more descriptive and discerning you can be about your feelings here, the more successful the process will be for you in the long run.

For example:

If I fail to let go of my ex, I will feel like I have let myself down and trapped in an unending cycle of pain and anger.

If I succeed in letting go of my ex, I will feel free to explore and participate in a fulfilling relationship with a new partner who appreciates me!

12. If possible, describe how you can combine the emotionally fulfilling situation you describe in questions 1, 2 and 3 with your new emotionally fulfilling/action/obstacle/solution/feeling scenario.

For example, if you love cooking, and finding a new partner would bring you joy, an action you could take would be to participate in a cooking class for singles. This way, you're already at a better emotional level when you're meeting new people because you're participating in an emotionally fulfilling activity.

2. Practice

Here begins the mental practice to achieve emotional fulfillment. It may seem this is redundant, but practice will give you the edge you need to achieve emotional health much more quickly than you may think is possible.

Begin by practicing mentally with the easiest action you chose that would bring you emotional fulfillment. See yourself implementing the solution you came up with that allows you to overcome the obstacle(s) that keep you from taking action. Imagine how you feel overcoming that obstacle. Next, see yourself taking the action(s) that bring you closer to achieving the result you desire. Imagine how you feel taking that action. Finally, see yourself achieving the emotional fulfillment you want and imagine how that feels.

If you are able to combine an existing emotionally fulfilling activity with your new actions (as you described in question 12 of planning), imagine participating in this activity.

3. Interaction

Now it's time to put your mental practice into action. Go back to your planning work and begin with the easiest to achieve action you can take to bring emotional fulfillment, take action, and observe your results – pay attention to positive or negative results, and pay particular attention to how you feel.

Once you've completed the first action, go through the rest and once again take note of your results and feelings.

4. Uniqueness

The uniqueness to pay attention to here is the change in emotions you will feel. That change in your outlook, mood and feelings are extremely valuable as this change puts you on the path to emotional well-being. You may achieve emotional health quickly, which will be exciting and easier than you expected. It may take time. If it takes time, focus on the changes you are accomplishing and be patient with yourself. Congratulate yourself on the progress you are making and look forward to your results improving.

For example: For me, having a sense of relief from the pain of losing Elaina was extremely unique and valuable to me because I was so entrenched in misery for so long.

5. Emotional Entanglement

You will notice in planning, practice and interaction, you have been discovering, imagining and observing how you want to be emotionally fulfilled instead of emotionally distressed. Your actions that bring you emotional fulfillment and how they intertwine with the emotional changes you desire will be what resolve your emotional distresses.

As you resolve your distresses, you will become emotionally entangled with the new situation you described only by focusing and feeling the way you desire instead of the way you used to feel. This will happen more quickly if you're able to combine existing emotionally fulfilling activities with new activities because they will reinforce each other.

Examine how you have felt in achieving the actions that are bringing you closer to emotional fulfillment and compare them with question 11 (If I fail/If I succeed question) in the planning section. Decide if your feelings have changed or if they've stayed the same now that you've gone through the process for the first time.

List anything(s) you can do to increase your excitement and/or fall in love with the fulfillment/action/obstacle/solution/feeling scenarios you're participating in to achieve your physical results.

6. Continuation

Set two dates and times where you will participate in the next round of fulfillment/action/obstacle/solution/feeling scenario. The first date and time will be for the next step (Evaluation) and then planning and practice. The second date and time will be to begin your next interaction where you follow through with your planning and practice.

As it was when working on the physical pillar of health, there are two steps in this process where people usually fail: 1 – getting yourself past the planning stage and 2 – coordinating continuation to evaluation. If you've read everything through but not answered the questions, go back and do it now. And schedule times for follow through on your planning, practice, and evaluation.

7. Evaluation

Now it's time to go over everything you've done and consider your results by asking yourself the following:

1. What are the unexpected challenges you faced by taking action to

achieve greater emotional fulfillment in your desired situation? List them.

2. Regarding these unexpected challenges, what can you do to overcome them? Who can you get help from to overcome them? How can you adjust your plans to be more successful?

3. Was there anything that surprised you about going through the process? What was it? Can you use this surprise to adjust your plans and be more successful?

4. In your planning, practice, and interaction with your goals, are there any results you want to add? Are there any results (now that you've tried obtaining them) that you want to remove?

5. Is the pursuit of your goals adding or taking away from your general wellbeing? Are they improving your relationship with yourself? Are they improving your relationships with others?

6. Are the results you desire truly contributing to your pillar of emotional health? Or are they actually a detriment?

7. Compare your results with your planning and practice. Does your plan need adjusting? Does your practice need adjusting? Does your interaction need adjusting? Does your uniqueness need to be more enticing for you to stay motivated? Does your emotional entanglement need to be stronger? What can you do to make your emotions stronger when it comes to your plan?

8. In all of this, are you being honest with yourself?

9. Are you pleased and delighted with your results so far? If not, what can you change in your plan to ensure you are happy?

10. Is there anything else you feel you should ask yourself and find the answer for, to ensure your success and emotional health? If there is ask yourself the question(s) and discover your answers.

Based on your answers to these questions, review and adjust your plan accordingly.

9.
The Fourth Pillar -
Manipulation of the Spiritual

In our world, there are many religions and faiths. This book is not here to tell you what to follow or believe. Provided your spiritual beliefs help you and others, it is your right as a human being to explore them in freedom, free from persecution. Strong spirituality can connect you with people, and being healthy spiritually gives many people comfort and hope.

Couples that share spirituality can have very powerful bonds and deep meaningful relationships; not only with their partners but in many other relationships in their life. Faith is a powerful motivator and channeled peacefully can be extremely beneficial. So, as you've explored and hopefully improved (or at least begun improving) your physical, mental and emotional health, it is worth exploring and improving your spiritual health as well.

There is beauty in faith. I have participated in Sunday morning gospel singing where the music is exhilarating and life affirming.

There is also destruction of faith. I've also seen the devastation that can be caused by extremists carrying out obliteration and annihilation justified in the name of faith.

Healthy faith and spirituality can be liberating and uplifting. Unhealthy faith and spirituality can be abhorrent.

What follows are questions I have asked myself, and my clients, to help improve relationships. These are also excellent questions to ask potential partners and have stimulating conversations when you are developing your relationships after your first dates.

Remember, you can obtain copies of these questions with space to write for free at:

http://www.manipulatethedate.com

1. Do you believe in God or a higher being or are you spiritual in some way? Describe what your answer means to you. If you believe, what does your belief mean to you? How does it affect your life? What actions do you take to further your beliefs? If you don't believe, what does your non-belief mean to you?

2. Is it important to you that your partner believes in God or a higher being or is spiritual in some way? Describe the qualities you would hope to see in your partner in this regard. What's the reason their faith or lack of faith is important to you? What do you perceive you will receive from them?

3. Do you practice spiritual/faith-based activities such as meditation, tai chi, yoga, etc.? What do you feel these activities contribute to your life?

4. What do you do to slow yourself down and reflect on your life?

5. What kinds of relationships do you have with other people of faith?

6. What kind of relationship do you have with atheists?

7. What do you think of extreme religious practices? How do they make you feel?

8. Have you ever contemplated a life in the clergy? What is your motivation to do so?

9. What books have you read to explore and learn about religion, faith and spirituality?

10. What kind of faith did your parents practice/experience? How have their practices/experiences influenced you?

11. Have you ever experienced the loss of a family member, friend, or loved one? If yes, what kinds of feelings did you experience during your loss? What kinds of thoughts did you have? Did your loss(es) bolster your spirituality/faith? Or did they reduce or remove the faith and spirituality that you had? If there was a change in your faith, what was the reasoning behind your change? Was the reasoning emotionally based? What were the emotions? Do you feel these emotions need resolving? (If so, go back to the last chapter and go through the emotional manipulation process outlined).

12. Do you contribute to the wellbeing of fellow human beings or the world? If so, how? If not, is there something you've always wanted to do to help others? For example, volunteer at a soup kitchen, or give blood, or buy a homeless person a meal, adopt a stray animal, or anything else where you expect no reward?

13. What kind of person are you? Do you perceive yourself as good? Are there areas of your life where you feel you could be a better person? What are they? What is one thing you could do right now to be a better person? Can you commit to doing that one thing?

14. Whether you are spiritual or an atheist, are there any spiritual leaders and/or organizations that you are disappointed in? What are the reasons they disappoint you? What is it they stand for that opposes your beliefs?

15. Whether you are spiritual or an atheist, are there any spiritual leaders and/or organizations that you respect or admire? What are the reasons you respect them? What is it they stand for that resonates with you?

16. Are there any religions, spiritual practices, places in the world you'd like to research, learn more about, or visit to explore your faith? Can you

make a plan to begin? If so, describe two or three actions you can take to begin your exploration.

10.
The Rules of
Manipulating the Date

Now that you're on the journey of manipulating yourself physically, mentally, emotionally, and spiritually to improve yourself and be a healthier person, you are ready to begin preparing yourself to Manipulate the Date with potential partners.

There are rules to manipulation. These rules will keep you and the people you connect with safe.

1. Be fun and interesting. When you are manipulating human interaction to have more successful relationships, it is your responsibility to make sure you and the people you're interacting with are having fun and that you are interesting. If you are being needy, or confrontational, or boring, or disrespectful, the people you meet will not become emotionally connected with you. If you can't emotionally connect, you can't create emotional entanglement and your interactions will be cut short and not happen again. When you are fun and interesting, people will naturally want to talk to you.

Think about it. When you're at a party, there's almost always someone who everyone wants to be around and talk to. Why is that? Because they're fun and interesting, and in some cases exciting. How can you tell if people find you fun and interesting? If they're having fun, they're usually laughing or smiling. When someone finds you interesting, they usually ask you questions and/or contribute to the conversation. If you're not sure, ask them if they're having fun or if they find what you're talking about interesting. If they don't find you fun and interesting, and actually admit it, you have the opportunity to save the date you're on by changing to a fun activity or talking about something they enjoy.

2. It's ok not to be perfect. Failure happens. Not every interaction results in emotional entanglement, not every first date results in continuation to another date. If someone does not like you or does not wish to see you again, do yourself a favor and get out and meet someone else. The easiest way to get over rejection is by meeting someone new, especially if you're following rule number 1: Be fun and interesting. When you're having fun and being interesting, you have something better to do than sit around and mope. You also increase your chances of success.

3. Be respectful. Treat your potential partners as you would want them to treat you. Manipulation is a powerful word that can be perceived negatively or positively depending on a person's viewpoint. If a person feels used or taken advantage of, they will feel negatively manipulated. Focus on the result you desire. If the result manipulates someone in a negative way, don't do it. It's simple; if you would take offense to someone manipulating you to achieve a result that is against your wishes, then odds are, they would not appreciate whatever you're doing either. This goes back to Rule 1: Be fun and interesting. In practice, you won't hear someone say, "I'm having too much fun and you're so interesting I feel used and taken advantage of." They are mutually exclusive.

To be respectful, think about how you wish someone else to treat you. How you wish to be treated is part of your standards and boundaries and you will use these standards to screen your potential partners as you get to know them. For example, I will not date a smoker (this includes vape-ing), but I will date a woman that enjoys the occasional cigar – I like cigars and have one about every 6 months or so and can appreciate someone that I can share the experience with. But a chain smoker is out. I have met women that smoke and I've had to friend zone them. Many have been intelligent, attractive, and potentially excellent partners. And regardless of their high qualities, I hate smoking and it's a deal breaker. For a non-smoker like me, kissing a smoker is like kissing an ashtray. Certainly, I will be friends and/or business associates with a smoker, but I will not date one.

Being respectful and defining your standards and boundaries so they are clear gives you a distinct advantage when you're pursuing any kind of relationship. It also sets you apart and makes you unique compared to most other people your potential partners meet. This is because people have not defined what they want in concrete detail.

Many people want to please someone else when they first meet, especially if they like them, and are afraid to express their opinion. Expressing your standards shows you are decisive and know what you want. This shows self-confidence and is attractive and makes you unique by comparison to others who are trying to please their date. This uniqueness makes you more desirable. Think about it for a moment. Who do you find more desirable and attractive? The person that knows what they want in life and has respect for himself or herself, or the needy person that would compromise his or her desires and date anyone that pays them the slightest attention?

It's vital to establish what you want from a partner before venturing into the dating world and meeting anyone. For both you and your potential partner, it saves time, effort and frustration when meeting. In the next chapter, Getting The First Date, there are exercises to establish your standards and boundaries.

4. Always ensure the person you are interacting with receives a benefit from your interaction. Leave them better than they were before you began the interaction. They will be better for having met you if you followed Rule #1 because you contributed something fun and interesting to their experience of life.

5. When the time comes to be intimate, ALWAYS have consent. There are multiple reasons for obtaining consent. I should not have to say this, but unfortunately, it still needs saying: If you don't have verbal AND physical consent, it's just plain wrong to be intimate with someone. Even when you have consent, your partner can withdraw it: Once you have verbal

consent, it is still your responsibility to always give your partner the option to stop at any time during physical interaction if they wish. If you don't have consent, you are no longer being fun, interesting, or respectful: You are committing sexual assault.

At this point, I encourage you to think about what you stand for morally and ethically. Describe your morals and ethics in detail especially how they relate to dating and your relationships. If you like, expand this exercise to include your family, work, business, and all other important aspects of your life. Be as descriptive as possible as this description will be important as you move forward and Manipulate the Date because it will give you the standards that are the cornerstone for ensuring that you treat your potential partners with respect, understanding, and dignity.

In addition to the beliefs you have about morals and ethics, the quality of the people you attract and cultivate relationships with will be directly proportional to the belief system you have about relationships.

Your belief system around dating and relationships is based on your upbringing, culture, experiences and is influenced by many things including how you choose to interpret and react to the following: Your parents' interactions, religious experiences, how your friends and other relationships interact, and your experiences interacting with people.

Usually, the more positive experiences you've had, the better you're able to react and interact with potential and current partners. Negative experiences can influence you as well, but only you know whether the influence is positive or negative. A negative experience like being cheated on can result in the choice to not trust a new partner. It can also result in the choice of trusting a new partner more profoundly because you realize you can give of yourself fully to someone that is faithful.

If you want a deeper understanding of how belief systems work, and how to manipulate and change them in a positive way, check out my book Success Through Manipulation: Subconscious Reactions That Will Make or Break You at:

http://www.stmbook.com

Many times, belief systems hold people back from being successful and if you feel you have negative beliefs that hold you back, that book will help you overcome them. As a bonus for buying this copy of Manipulate the Date, you can enter the following promo code on the website to get 50% off the PDF electronic version.

MTDBELIEF

6. In dating, all things are possible. I have seen people that you would never think to have anything in common get together and have great dates and fantastic relationships.

For example, the adage, "Like attracts like," is a useful belief, but it's also limiting depending on your perspective. Certainly, if you are physically fit, the odds are in your favor that you are more attractive to another fit person. The chances of meeting another fit person increase substantially when you go a to a gym, a yoga studio or other places where fit people gather.

This is not to say that if you're not fit, you're precluded from dating someone that is fit; it's just more likely to happen faster and have a greater probability of succeeding if you're both fit.

I have a friend, Ursula, who dated a fitness trainer Greg. They both worked on a cruise ship together. Greg was Joe six-pack and Ursula was about 70 pounds overweight when they met. They socialized together after work, and it turned out he really liked her and loved spending time with her. He saw past her weight and they began dating. He said he would never be attracted to someone that was overweight, and she always said, "I'm always going to be fat."

What's amazing for her, within about six months, she lost all her extra weight and felt (and looked) amazing. Their relationship flourished for almost two years. In fact, I'm pretty sure they'd still be together except they stopped working on cruise ships. They lived in different countries and couldn't see each other because neither wanted to move. Proximity is important for relationships to continue.

If you have limiting beliefs about dating, start telling yourself every day: "All things are possible!"

11.
Getting the First Date

Now you know the rules and it's time to start planning.

The initial planning and practice phases in the next chapter will be the longest because there is a great deal of information for you to think about, learn and prepare.

Remember, you can obtain copies of these questions for free on my website at:

http://www.manipulatethedate.com

Planning - Discovering What You Want

1. List a potential partner's qualities that are absolute deal breakers. These are qualities or habits that would stop you cold from pursuing them for a romantic relationship. Your list could include a smoker, drug user, alcoholic, gambler, an abusive person, someone who scrapes their fingernails across hard surfaces to make an annoying high pitch sound, or other really bad habits.

2. List the qualities and traits of a potential partner that may aggravate you but are not deal breakers. For example: Not putting the toilet seat down, doesn't eat all their vegetables, or snores. Ok, maybe snoring might not be a deal breaker for you, but you get the idea.

3. List must-have qualities of a potential partner – wanting children or being a vegan, for example.

4. List the qualities of a potential partner that would be nice to have, but are not necessarily a must have. For example: Maybe you'd like them to own their own home, but it's ok if they're renting right now. Maybe you have a secret Oreo obsession and it would be great if they brought you milk and cookies in bed... unless you're lactose intolerant: Gassing your partner after they bring you milk and cookies is just mean! □

5. Have a little fun and describe the perfect day with a partner who has all your "must have qualities" and your "nice to have qualities" and describe

how you would feel after participating in this wonderful day.

Now that you have a much better idea of the kind of partner you're looking for, it's time to show your date the qualities that they are looking for. Whether your date has their own list or not, on a subconscious level, they are looking to see that you are a partner of substance and has qualities they find valuable and attractive. These next questions will give you some tools to convey your uniqueness to your date.

Planning - Discovering What You Can Give

6. Other than looks, list 10 qualities that make you attractive to a potential mate and describe why each quality is desirable. If you have more than 10, list as many as you can. If you're having trouble getting to 10, ask your friends or coworkers to help you make your list. Many people sell themselves short here and feel they have few worthwhile qualities. You actually do and you'll be pleasantly surprised when you ask your friends and coworkers and they tell you.

7. Of the 10 qualities from the previous question, choose the top three that you would like to communicate with the person you go on a date with. For each of these qualities, think about a story from your life you can tell that illustrates each particular quality. On a blank sheet of paper, write the story out in one to two pages. Then read it out loud and time it. It should not take you more than two to three minutes to recite the story. If it takes longer, edit it down. The idea is to have stories that show your date the kind of person you are in an engaging yet indirect way. The story can involve any emotion, but as you write three stories, have two fun ones, and a third that shows some vulnerability so your date knows you have the ability to be serious as well as fun. Eventually, you will want to have stories from your life for all 10 qualities, and if you have time, write the stories out for all 10. But it's ok to start with three and come back during continuation to decide how to augment your plan and what you need to practice next. As you're writing, you may notice some stories illustrate multiple qualities. That's great! In fact, the best stories are ones

that show you in different ways.

Here's one of my stories:

When I was working on cruise ships, one of my favorite places I visited was Naples, Italy. It's my favorite because when I was about seven or eight we studied Pompeii in school, and Naples is the gateway to Pompeii. It was scary in that these people were burned alive in an instant, but at the same time I was fascinated with how the city was preserved by lava from the volcano. I always wanted to visit and see this city frozen in time for humanity to discover two thousand years later. I remember sailing into Naples and looking at Vesuvius taunting me across the water. Walking through the ruins was soooo cool – much different than what I learned about it when I was a kid.

One of the things that surprised me most was they were in the middle of an election and there was advertising on the walls of the candidates for mayor. I was also blown away when I looked at the street and could see sections of underground piping popping out. They actually had plumbing then. The tour guide even took us to the local brothel where they had different rooms with different "activities" and you could decide what you wanted from a "Lady of Pompeii" by looking at a picture above the door – they conveniently neglected to tell us about that in elementary school. It was a dream come true for me! Seeing Pompeii… not the brothel!

This is a great story that everyone loves. I can tell it at any time on a date, during networking, or with friends at a bar. It is not date specific. These are the reasons it is a good story:

A. The story shows the following qualities: I like to travel. I'm adventurous. I like to learn about history. I can make a joke.

B. It sets up further conversation by paving the way for follow-up questions that allow my date to express their own opinion and experiences. I can ask:

i) Have you ever visited a place you dreamed of seeing as a child?

ii) Have you ever been on a cruise ship?

iii) What's your take on the fact that they never taught about the brothels in elementary school?

iv) Can you believe civilization was advanced enough to have plumbing 2000 years ago?

v) What do you think those people felt as they were trapped in Pompeii with minutes to live?

In addition to follow-up questions, there are follow-up topics, including Italian food in Naples. This topic can branch out into stories of favorite restaurants.

C. The story shows emotional excitement (much more so as I tell it than as it's written) and shows I'm comfortable expressing emotion. The excitement is contagious and allows for emotional connection because the people I tell it to also get excited.

D. Listeners like it because it is true and it shows that I am open to talking about my childhood.

E. It separates me from other people my date has met, because honestly, how many people actually talk about fulfilling a dream they had as a child? In all my dates, there are only three that I remember hearing. Unfortunately, many people don't fulfill their dreams and meeting someone who has achieved a childhood dream is usually impressive (especially when you tell the story in a way that portrays your enthusiasm and excitement).

Planning - Deciding Where You Will Begin Meeting Potential Dates

There are many places to meet potential partners. I'll start with places to avoid and then I'll give you places with much more potential for success in dating.

Avoid singles nights (unless it's a singles dancing night), singles bars, singles speed dating, or anything with the word "singles" in the advertising. Admittedly, there are many nice people who go to these kinds of "singles" events. However, I have found the people who attend are generally newly single or have been single for a very long time and desperate for a relationship. These are qualities to avoid.

What are the reasons to avoid dating people like this? People who are newly single are difficult to date because they are still emotionally compromised by their breakup and their change in lifestyle. There is a time of grieving and, in general, until the person has properly grieved, you will become the brunt of their past relationship issues with their ex. You'll be the rebound.

People who are desperate for a relationship tend to look for a partner that will fill their void of loneliness. This makes them difficult to date because it is a terrible focus to have when looking for a relationship partner. Because their interactions with you cannot be focused on creating a meaningful relationship, their attention will be centered on ensuring they alleviate their loneliness. Save yourself a great deal of drama and stick with people who are happy by themselves and will compliment your fun.

If you decide to participate in singles events, bear in mind that because your focus is to be fun and interesting, you will be very popular at the event. Concentrate on looking for the other fun and exciting singles and don't get your time and energy bogged down with negative people.

If you are newly out of a relationship or you feel desperate and/or lonely, go back and work on your 4 pillars of health from earlier in this book. That way, you'll create the right frame of mind to be a positive contributor to an incredible relationship with a healthy person. Your relationship partners deserve your best, just as you deserve their best.

Unless you're brand new to dating or ended a long relationship and have not dated in a long time, the next place to avoid is Internet dating. Considering the descriptions of my adventures in Internet dating, you may be surprised at this statement. You'll recall the Internet was an excellent place for me to begin and develop the Manipulate the Date process. Now if you experience similar social issues and anxiety like I did, then by all means start with the Internet. Here's why I believe you'll be more successful spending your time elsewhere:

As you recall, after I broke up with Elaina and spent four years depressed, I worked on my 4 pillars of health. When I was ready to date again, I created new Internet dating profiles. As I began the process anew, the Internet took on a tone of bitterness for me. Unlike before, I was no longer the robot who sent out emails and set up coffee dates. Yes, I could easily do it. The process still worked well, but it felt horrible to do. I had grown past the insecure man that couldn't talk to strangers into a man that could strike up a fun and interesting conversation almost anywhere at any time. I knew something was missing. So I analyzed the problem and here's what I observed:

It is correct that many people meet online and have successful relationships. According to match.com, one in five relationships start online. eHarmony says they are responsible for over 1 million marriages and I'm sure other Internet sites have all kinds of great statistics to sell their products. I've used both these sites and others and they are excellent tools to meet people.

Their statistics for creating relationships are impressive … until you flip them around or compare them to other relevant statistics. One in five relationships starting online flipped around means four in five relationships start offline. That means 80% of relationships start offline. In the United States alone (according to CDC.gov) there are over two million marriages every year compared to one million marriages over eHarmony's entire lifetime around the world. That's a very small number compared to the number of marriages that occur worldwide every year.

The Ashley Madison scandal in 2015 has shown that many Internet profiles on their website were fake robots created by programmers. To be clear, I do not promote or condone infidelity. If you use this book to be a cheater, I say, "Stop being an asshole!" Break up with your partner and allow them the dignity of moving on with someone who respects them enough to be faithful.

There is enough relationship pain in the world without deliberate cheaters hurting their partners. If you are a person looking for a committed monogamous relationship, I recommend you focus your efforts on single and eligible partners, but I am using the Ashley Madison scandal as an example because Internet dating sites will not come forward stating that some sites have fake profiles.

Here's a link to an article detailing this assertion:

http://www.salon.com/2015/08/31/the_very_human_secret_of_ashley_madisons_fembot_success/

This following is a quote from one of the code experts, Annalee Newitz from the article in the link above:

"What I have learned from examining the site's source code is that Ashley Madison's army of fembots appears to have been a sophisticated, deliberate, and lucrative fraud. The code tells the story of a company trying to weave the illusion that women on the

site were plentiful and eager. Whatever the total number of real, active female Ashley Madison users is, the company was clearly on a desperate quest to design legions of fake women to interact with the men on the site."

It's been my experience that all Internet dating sites I have used have fake profiles of some kind. There are plenty of sites I have not used so it's possible some have all real people with legitimate profiles. Sometimes fake profiles are webcam scammers trying to make money. Sometimes it's fake profiles of scammers from other countries trying to get you to send them money. Sometimes it's robots created by the sites computer programmers.

With the experience I've had, it's easy for me to spot fake profiles – especially once a conversation thread starts. But to someone with little to no computer dating or technology experience, it can be difficult. Admittedly, some of the sites allow you to report fake profiles and do their best to delete fakes when they are discovered. But even so, 15 to 20% of responses I've received online are from fake profiles as I've described.

Also, with online dating, there is a great deal of competition, window shopping, and serial daters not interested in creating relationships.

So with statistics and fraud staring me in the face, I realized it was time to get off the computer and out into the real world. That being said, if you've had good success with online dating or want to try it, you can meet great people there, and if you feel it's right for you, use the Internet. But as you use it, if you find it's not working, let it go. Remember four in five relationships (80%) still start offline. That's what I was missing. I was focused on the hardest 20% instead of the abundant 80%.

If you decide to use the Internet to get first dates, here are some guidelines to follow to increase your chances of success:

i) **Be honest!** – Real age, smoking habits, number of children (if you have them) and real pictures. If you lie, your date will find out and be thoroughly pissed off at you and you'll have to start over. Healthy relationships are based on honesty and trust. If you lie from the start, you are sabotaging yourself.

ii) Have recent pictures – 3 months or less. If you're online longer than 3 months, update your pictures. You want to post sharp photos, but ones where you look even better in person! From the perspective of the person you want to meet, it's frustrating meeting someone that doesn't look like their pictures because they feel like you're misrepresenting yourself and it diminishes your chances of a 2nd date substantially.

iii) Have at least three pictures – headshot, full body activity shot, and a third of your choice. Do not have other people in your pictures unless the full body activity shot is something that requires a partner, i.e. dancing. Make sure if other people are in the photo, the person viewing your profile can easily tell which one is you.

iv) No pictures of you in the bathroom. Seriously, do you think that bathroom stall behind you is going to make you look hot? Oh right… No romance like toilet romance! God, I hope you washed your hands before taking a picture of your reflection in the mirror right after taking that turd… oops look in the bowl, forgot to flush and your big log is in your profile picture… YES, I've seen thousands of Internet dating profiles and I cannot un-see the nasties I have seen.

v) Photos with cats. Don't do them! This goes for other animals too – alive or dead. The person looking at your profile wants to date you, not your cat! It's ok to have a separate picture of your pet on its own, but don't turn yourself into the Internet cat lady. I'll say it a second time in case you missed it. No dead animals in your dating profile pictures!

vi) If you have children, don't include pictures of them in your profile. This is for their protection!

vii) Stay away from selfies and bathing suit pictures. These kinds of pictures attract people who are looking for one night stands. If that's what you're looking for, then by all means go for it. But if you're looking for a quality partner for a date avoid these. What's a person's motivation to post these types of pictures? It's been my experience that they're usually looking for validation, not a relationship. Men and women who post these kinds of pictures tend to be needy and are hard to be in a relationship with. They gravitate to the people online that give them the most attention. As soon as someone else gives them more attention they'll drop you for that next person.

viii) Read profiles of your competition and see what they are saying about themselves and craft something that sets you apart. If you need help, get a friend to help you.

ix) Run your profile through a spell checker and keep it to 1000 words or less (some sites let you go longer and some shorter). No abbreviations, like "I'm luking 4 U & want gud relatunshep."

x) Sometimes you get what you pay for, other times not. On free dating websites like plentyoffish.com and Tinder there are many more men and fewer women. Because they're free, men get lost in the shuffle and women get inundated with messages and many times sexually harassed or belittled. As a man I feel it is unacceptable for you to belittle or sexually harass women online or in person. Women deserve respect. As a woman, you'll have to be patient, sift through the douchebags, and look for the good guys. My girlfriends that participate in online dating seem to get about 20 messages from men to my every one message a man may receive from a woman. So as a woman, if you like a man, send him a message. The odds are good he'll respond because no one else is talking to him. On paid websites men have a better chance of standing out with a good profile because competition is less and women don't get as inundated by as many creeps. Before paying for anything, check out the profiles first. If all the people you like are on the free sites, save your money and opt for the free site. If all the people you're interested in are on the paid sites only, go to the paid sites – again beware of fake profiles. Who is on what site will vary geographically so take some time and research a few to determine which is best for you before spending any money.

xi) I've said this before and I'll say it again. Be respectful of the people you speak to. As a man online, there will be lots of rejection. Don't take out your hurt feelings on the next woman you talk to. As a woman, if you're not interested in a man, be honest and tell them you're not interested. If he becomes a jerk, report and block him.

Work can be a great place to meet someone. The challenge is, if your relationship is unsuccessful, you may still have to work with them and that may create stress. If your relationship is successful, you may also see them all day and then all night. Some people flourish in this scenario. Others don't. You'll have to decide what's best for you. If you're not sure, avoid dating people from work.

So the question is, how do the other 80% of relationships begin? Some of my favorite places to meet people are art nights, cooking classes, meet up groups, Karaoke nights, amateur sports you can participate in, dance classes and dance nights. Others places relationships start are at friends' parties or blind dates friends set you up on, bookstores, grocery stores, coffee shops, malls, university and college campuses, poetry nights, concerts, comedy nights, open mic nights, awards nights, volunteering at charities, special interest clubs, and group travel destinations. Basically, anywhere you have the opportunity to have fun and can naturally talk to someone. Mix it up and cultivate different options and see which ones you like best and which ones work best for you.

8. Think about the places or events the kind of person you want to meet would go to and socialize in their daily lives. List them and schedule times in your calendar to go to these places with the idea to participate and have fun and socialize. Depending on your comfort level talking to strangers, you may find it easier to take part in the many places and things to do mentioned in the paragraph above. There you can speak to people on a repeated basis and use the repeated activity as an opportunity to talk comfortably. If you're shy, talk to people who are obviously in a relationship or married and make friends with them first. You will feel no dating pressure from someone already in a relationship and it will naturally be easier to speak. Even if there is no one you would consider dating at the event you're participating in, when you make friends with good people (and they like you), they almost always know single people that they can set you up with. In the next section, you will begin planning fun dates. You can always invite couples you are friends with to the events

you plan, and you can encourage them to invite single friends. If you can show them you're fun and interesting and they like you, they will recommend you to their single friends and help you be more successful. Usually, when I go to events myself, I immediately look for a couple and begin a conversation with them first because it creates social validation. The rest of the people in the room now see me as fun and interesting. It's easy, unexpected, and sets me apart from other single people who are wallflowers or hitting on people directly without the social validation my new friends provide to the subconscious perception of everyone else around me.

9. Make a list of friends you can invite to these places or events. It's perfectly acceptable to go alone. Some people find it more comfortable to go with a friend. Of the people you list, choose the top three that you feel will help you meet people. If you feel no one that can assist you on the list, then go to the events yourself.

Planning - Researching Fun Locations to Have in Your Back Pocket: Having a Plan Before You Go Out and Meet People

The easiest way to ask someone out on a first date is to not actually ask them out on a date. Instead, ask them to a planned fun activity. This greatly increases the chances that the person will spend precious time talking to you.

10. List five places where you've gone, or want to go to, where fun activities happen. The activities should be different from the run of the mill. If you have no budget or are low on funds, it's great to do free things. For example, amateur mic nights are usually free and are a great source for conversation; other interesting things can be wall climbing, art galleries, a great hole in the wall dive restaurant with eclectic atmosphere, etc. If you're having trouble, most cities have a newspaper or magazine with upcoming local events (many of them free) you can use for ideas. Now research a coffee shop nearby each of these places (preferably a short walking distance). You will use both locations to set up 2-part dates. First the coffee shops to meet, and then if things are going well, the next activity where you can walk over and have fun.

When you are ready to go out and meet people, schedule five places over the next two weeks. When you're talking to people, you can tell them about what you're going to be doing and if you feel they are people you want to get to know better, you can easily invite them because the activities and places are researched. Notice I said you will invite them if you want to get to know them. As the person who is fun and interesting, you will have the ability to choose who you spend your time with on your fun and interesting adventures. Being able to choose who you get to know and spend time with is powerful and creates self- confidence.

As you invite people, always plan on going whether they say yes or not. Simply put, even if you go yourself, you will have the opportunity to meet people at the locations you go to. Earlier in the book I talked about how often I was stood up for a date. Many times, instead of sitting and moping, I would start talking to people where I was. If you don't feel you're ready to invite someone single on a date, plan to go with friends or the couples you met earlier (see question 8).

Planning - Having Something Interesting To Talk About: Never Run Out of Conversation Material

11. Go to your favorite social media website and look at the top three to five trending topics. Study them so you can talk about them with people you meet. When there is a pause in the conversation, you will have three to five conversation starters - very helpful if you're nervous or you don't know what to say.

For example, if it's election time, you can talk about the candidate(s) you like or who they like. You could say, "I was reading earlier that Super Sally is leading in the polls. What do you think of her?"

12. As you study the trending topics, create a statement and question sentence for each of the topics you chose in one of the following formats:

I was reading online earlier that _____ is _____. What do you think of that?

Or

I heard that _____ is _____. What's your take on that?

For example, "I was reading online earlier that some processed foods are linked to cancer. What do you think of that?"

You can also choose your own format. The structure is a statement of any topic followed by an open-ended question to get their opinion.

Once you have some sentences and topics, also be sure that you have your own opinions about the topics that you can communicate. Otherwise the conversation will be too one sided.

Usually, I spend five minutes reading about each topic so I'm knowledgeable enough to talk about the subject. You don't have to be an expert, just know enough to be able to ask a few questions of the people you meet and have an interesting conversation.

13. In the same format as the previous question, create three to five statement/question sentences of your own that are timeless.

For example:

• "I was reading about climate change the other day and scientists are predicting some islands will eventually disappear and be covered in water. What do you think about climate change?"

• "I heard NASA has plans to colonize Mars in the 2030s. What do you think about that? Do you think humanity could survive and thrive on Mars?"

• "A friend of mine found out her husband was cheating on her and asked me what she should do. What do you think is the best advice to give her?"

Use those or think of your own. As you create your own, think about events that have happened in your life that were dramatic to create your statements and then ask questions of your date that get their opinion on the topic. Avoid yes/no answer questions. You want questions that are open ended so the conversation can be expanded on.

Planning - How to Present Yourself: Clothing and Hygiene

This is a very broad topic that changes over time with fashion. I am not a fashion expert or image consultant. So instead, I will give you some general principles for you to examine your wardrobe and your lifestyle to determine how to present yourself for the best success.

The old adage "Dress for Success" is as important in the dating world as it is at work. In the dating world, looks do matter but not in the way most people think. Being well groomed and put together is more important than your overall attractiveness. As a woman, if you're drop dead gorgeous, or you're a very handsome man, that certainly helps in the beginning, but as you progress in the date, looks will take a back seat to being fun, interesting and being able to display your uniqueness and emotionally connect.

A few months ago, I had gone on four dates with a very attractive woman, Rhonda. She decided she wanted to be with her roommate who is an overweight, socially awkward guy. On our dates, she was very adamant that she only dated physically fit men. She could easily have her choice of many good-looking, fit suitors. But, when it came down to it, she had lived with her roommate for over a year and had formed an emotional entanglement with him that overrode her idea of physical attraction. He asked her out to dinner and she accepted and declined to go out with me again.

Looks aren't everything. It's the combination of your looks, your uniqueness, and the emotional entanglement you have with your date that determines your success. But being well groomed and presentable indeed make it easier!

Depending on your financial situation, you may be at the height of fashion, you may not be. As a man, it's important to have nice shoes. Women notice them. As for the rest of your clothing whether you're a man or a woman, make sure your clothing is clean and fits you properly. A shirt that is $5 at a thrift store can usually be tailored for between $5 and $25 depending where you are geographically and will look better tailored to fit your body than a $100 untailored shirt. The same goes for pants and other clothing. Go hang out at a mall or other high traffic location and notice the people who have clothing that fit them well usually look much better than people that don't. It's not that they're more or less attractive, it's that they're presenting themselves well in clothing that fits. Even if you're overweight, you will look better in well-fitting clothing than you do wearing clothes that fit you poorly. Spend your money on a tailor before spending money on new clothing.

When it comes to good hygiene. Have it. Bad breath is a huge turn off! Brush your teeth before any date and use breath mints when you need them. If you're not sure your breath is good, ask your friends if you generally have good or bad breath and adjust your oral care accordingly. If you're on a date and you're not sure of your breath, err on the side of caution and gobble down a mint.

Wear deodorant and/or antiperspirant if you need it. If you're not sure, you need it… wear it! Be as clean as possible. Avoid overpowering perfumes and colognes. Just because you like the smell of something does not mean your date will. Side note, going to a perfume/cologne store and smelling samples on each other can be an interesting date.

Smokers – Quit. You've heard it before. Do it for your health. But beyond that, you also stink and if you're meeting a non-smoker it's a turn off. Even if you're meeting another smoker, many won't date another smoker, especially if they're trying to quit. Do yourself a favor and quit. If you need help, get my stop smoking hypnosis recordings at

http://www.hypnosishealthstore.com

14. Go through your wardrobe and choose your three favorite outfits. These are clothes that fit you well, look good on you, increase your self-confidence, and are appropriate for the locations and activities you have chosen. As you choose your outfits, examine them to make sure they are in good repair and if they need to be tailored to look better on you, get them tailored and ready for when you need them.

15. If after looking at your wardrobe you do not feel you have appropriate clothing, go out and buy it. If you're low on funds, thrift stores and factory outlets have great bargains if you go looking. If you're not sure what to buy, ask a friend with fashion sense to help you. Communicate with the friend that you are looking to buy clothing that will help you feel attractive to potential partners and will fit you well and make you look good.

Planning - Prepare Your Sanctuary

When it comes to where you live, it must be clean. At some point, you will be inviting your potential partner to your place.

One night I was the designated driver. One of my friends, Lance, met a really nice woman at the bar. She was intelligent, articulate and they got along famously. She liked him, he liked her and she invited him over to her place. They were consenting adults. Twenty minutes after he left the bar with her, Lance phoned me and said, "OMG! Colin, come pick me up. Her place is fucking disgusting. There's a layer of garbage halfway up my shins in the living room. There's moldy pizza on the couch and it stinks."

Have a clean place or you will drive potential partners away.

16. Make a cleaning schedule for your place and stick to it so that it's ready for company to visit. If you don't do it, hire a cleaning person. In the long run, the success of your dating life will depend on how comfortable your potential partner feels in your place. Prepare it properly so it's inviting.

Practice

Up until now, everything you've been planning and working on is predicated on being able to talk to people and socialize. Maybe you're already confident at starting conversations with people; maybe you're not. Whether you are confident or not, the following information and exercises will help you practice and increase your confidence and help you start conversations.

Keep in mind with the planning you've done so far, you've made more progress than most people. You now have:

- Locations and activities where you can meet potential partners
- Date ideas planned for once you do
- Conversation topics you've researched
- Opinions on your topics to keep conversations going

This is powerful because you don't have to worry about not knowing what to do once you have the date set up. This reduces the pressure on you. Instead of you and your potential partner feeling awkward about the date you can focus on having fun and getting to know each other.

For example, remember earlier in the book I told you when I was 14 I asked out Maria saying, "I heard you want to go out with me?" This scenario was a set up for failure for many reasons, but one of the main reasons was because I had no activity to ask her to participate in. If I had planned ahead of time and remembered that she liked soccer I could have asked her to a soccer game. Imagine if I had walked up to her and said, "Hey Maria, there's a soccer game after school on Wednesday. Let's watch it together."

That simple scenario would have allowed Maria to say either, "Yes" or "I have other plans for Wednesday." At that point if she had liked me (which I knew she did) and said no to watching soccer, she was rejecting the idea of the activity instead of me or the idea of going on a date. I could have planned something else and asked again without the awkwardness. In fact, it would have started the conversation on a positive note and all we would have had to do was plan logistics of when to go out. With five activities planned over a two-week span, you have multiple opportunities to ask a potential date to an event they can participate in. In addition, they will see that you are a person that is active and social that can add to their life.

So you now have the focus of meeting someone with the idea that you will be able to participate in fun and interesting experiences with the people you meet instead of asking to go out with no idea how to have fun, or even worse, asking them to go on a potentially boring dinner and movie date.

Speaking of dinner and movie dates. As a rule of thumb, don't do them until you've had at least four successful fun and interesting dates beforehand. Even if your potential partner says their favorite thing to do is watch movies, wait until after the 4th date. A dinner-movie is an unintentional dating pitfall! In a movie, you can't talk to your date. Neither of you can communicate your awesome qualities sitting in the dark watching a movie in silence. The exception might be dinner and a movie at home where you cook together, and it's a lovely evening where you can build emotional entanglement with a movie to relax and watch after an excellent meal and stimulating conversation.

Interaction Practice

I had just finished a show in Jasper, Alberta, Canada, and I was invited for drinks at the Athabasca hotel bar. One of the volunteers in my show was excited to introduce me to a woman he was good friends with.

He did his introductions and as I extended my hand to shake hers, she punched me square in the privates and skipped away. As I dropped to the ground in agony, the locals laughed.

Once I recovered, I asked the guy, "Why the hell did she do that?"

He said, "Oh, that's just what she does. We introduce everyone to her for fun. It's like a right of passage for your testicles!"

It was a "right" I could have lived with out...

If you have confidence issues, rest assured you won't get punched in the privates (unless you meet that woman in Jasper). But in case you're anxiety makes you feel like the worst could happen, the following exercises will help you be more confident, and have a game plan to interact and be ready to start meeting people. Remember, you have some trending conversation topics you researched in the planning section so you will always have something to say.

Once you are comfortable talking to strangers, you'll be ready to go to the places you researched in the planning stage to begin meeting potential partners.

Ideally you are looking for ways to practice starting your interactions with people. When you're able to start conversations quickly, you will move onto the next step where interactions to meet potential partners begin.

1. Go back to your planning and memorize the three stories you wrote (question 7 in planning) that demonstrate the qualities you want to communicate to a potential date. This was why they were to be kept short between two to three minutes to facilitate easy memorization. If they're too long, edit them down again so they're shorter and still get the major points of the story and the qualities you want to portray across. Next, memorize the conversation starters and conversation topic statement/ questions (questions 11, 12 and 13 in planning) that you created. Next, memorize the five locations/activities that you researched and added to your calendar (question 10 in planning). The goal of memorization is not to be a robot. The goal is to be able to recall the stories and conversation topics when you're under pressure meeting people. That way you're able to talk about the fun activities you have planned and can invite potential dates to while easily keeping your wits about you.

2. With your stories and topics memorized, go to a food court in a busy mall and find a long line where people are waiting. As you're standing in line say the following to the person/people waiting in line in front of you:

"While we're waiting, let me get your take on something. My friend wants to surprise his girlfriend and buy her a puppy. They've been living together for a while and he thinks it will bring their relationship to the next level. So my question is, "Do you think it's better for the relationship if he discusses it with her first? Or is it better to buy the puppy and surprise her?"

Listen to their answer. Give your viewpoint and say thank you. Then, you can continue talking or you can say, "Thanks for your help. I appreciate it. I'm going to go call him now and let him know what I think." You can leave then. Remember, the idea is not to get a date. You are practicing talking to strangers so you become comfortable socializing. You're doing it in a food line up at the mall because it's a natural location where people would normally engage in idle chit chat to pass the time. Instead of talking about the weather, you're going to talk about an interesting topic that most if not all people have an opinion on. Talk to both men and women and talk to groups of people where possible and get everyone's opinion. This will give you the practice to be able to speak confidently when you're at locations where you are specifically looking for someone to date.

You don't have to use the puppy question. You can use any of the conversation topics you came up with in the planning section, but this statement/question combination usually gets people talking because people like to talk about altering relationship dynamics and pets are usually a fun topic for many.

Repeat this process five to ten times until you are comfortable talking to random strangers in line. It does not matter whom you talk to in line. It only matters that you get used to talking to random people. If, after five to ten times, you still don't feel comfortable, repeat the exercise until you do. You can do this over the span of a few days. It took me over 50 times before I was comfortable. If conversation progresses, you will have other topics to generate conversation if you choose to continue. I always got out of line before we got to the front so I didn't have to buy anything. If you are having an interesting conversation that's great: Keep interacting. You don't have to stop.

3. Going back to question 10 of the planning step where you chose five fun locations/activities and choose one you like. As you did in the first exercise, go to a food court and wait in a long line and strike up a conversation. This time, you will start the conversation by talking about the location/activity that you chose. Format your initial interaction with a statement about the location/activity and follow it with an open-ended question that seeks their opinion.

For example, if your location/activity is skydiving you could say to the person in line, "While we're waiting, have you ever been skydiving? I'm jumping out of a plane for the first time next week and I'm really excited!

Maybe a bit scared. Have you ever been skydiving? What do you think is the scariest part?"

Listen to their answer. Give your viewpoint and say thank you. You can keep talking or you can say, "Thanks for your perspective. I appreciate it. At this point, you can leave. If you're not sure how to leave just say, "I think I want something else to eat from over there." After you say that it will seem natural that you walk away. You can enter another lineup and start another conversation. Remember, the idea here is not to get a date. You are practicing talking to strangers about the fun activities you have planned. As before, talk to both men and women and talk to groups of people where possible and get everyone's opinion. This will give you the practice to be able to talk about your fun activities when you're at locations where you are specifically looking for someone to date. Do this five to ten times or more if you need so you feel comfortable talking about your fun activities. If you feel you need to do this exercise more, do more. It's ok. You can also spread this out over a few days if you need more time to practice.

In the continuation step coming up, you will learn how to invite someone to your location/event. For now, practice talking about your activities in an exciting way.

Real World Interaction, Uniqueness, and Emotional Entanglement

It's time to take your planning and practice into the real world. Your confidence level and your social skills will determine where to begin. Go back to question 8 in the planning section where you researched where your potential dates would be located or participating in activities. Choose one, go there, and start talking to people. The location/activity you choose first will be the one where you feel most comfortable talking to people in a natural setting.

As examples, if you're meeting people in a dance class, you'll be talking about your dance class and sprinkling in conversation. If you're meeting at an art night, the natural conversation will be about art. Always ensure your conversation partially revolves around the location and activity you are participating in/at because it's natural to talk about that when you're there and it makes the people you're talking to feel comfortable.

Starting the conversation should be relatively easy for you at this point provided you completed the planning and practice exercises in the previous section. You will have four goals you want to focus on. Memorize these goals now before going out and interacting:

i) **Show your uniqueness** – What makes you fun and interesting and worth spending time with? Your conversational topics that are different from other people and your stories that display your good qualities show your uniqueness. Focus on transitioning from casual chit-chat about the current location/activity to showing your uniqueness to the people you are speaking to.

ii) Build emotional entanglement – Focus on beginning to build emotional connections with the people you are talking to. If you have told your stories well and had interesting conversations, you will have communicated your uniqueness properly. They will naturally begin to emotionally connect with you. With enough emotional connections, it's natural that the people you interact with will want to spend more time with you.

iii) Talk about the future activities you have planned. You're not inviting anyone to them; you're just talking about how you're looking forward to them. Be brief. For example, if you're going skydiving next week, use the statement/conversation starter that you came up with: "Have you ever been skydiving? I'm going next week! I'm a bit scared. Do you think it's ok to be scared?" or "I'm going to the new bodyworks art exhibit tomorrow. I love how beautiful the human body can be. What do you think about the exhibit?"

iv) Make sure you listen to them. Conversation is a 2-way street. Let them talk as much as possible and discover all you can about them. Ensure they feel comfortable talking to you as you listen.

With your interactions started and you using your conversation topics and stories about yourself where you need them, you will automatically be displaying your uniqueness. This is uniqueness compared to everyone else they're talking to. Many people will have difficulty socializing in a fun and interesting way because they are unprepared to do so. You are the exception with all the preparation you've put into ensuring interesting conversation.

This is what makes you unique and will allow you to hold their attention and engage them. Your second display of uniqueness will be when you tell your stories that you wrote and memorized (question 7 from planning). If you've done this correctly, you will have two fun stories that show distinct qualities about yourself and convey emotion. You will also have a vulnerable story that demonstrates that you can be serious. These stories, when delivered correctly, will emotionally connect the people you're talking with to you while displaying the qualities you've highlighted in the story.

Continuation

So you've displayed your uniqueness and begun to emotionally connect with people using your stories. As conversations progress, it will be time to set up your next date with the person you're talking to. Remember, as you're talking, evaluate if they are a match to the qualities you said you desire in a partner (questions 1 through 5 in planning). For example, if you don't want to date a smoker and they smoke, don't invite them to spend more time with you. It's ok to be selective. It's also ok to just be friends with someone. Remember, a good friend has the potential to set you up with one of their friends. And good friends are just plain important to have anyway.

To ask them out to a future location/activity, you must have already talked about that activity earlier. If you haven't talked about that location/activity, you must continue the conversation until you have. Then continue the conversation more and circle back when you've communicated more uniqueness and gained more emotional connection. Then ask when you feel it's appropriate. If you're not sure when it's appropriate that's ok, the way you will ask will take care of that. Remember, it's better to talk about the location/activity earlier on in the conversation and gotten their opinion about it and move onto other topics so you have lots of time to naturally display uniqueness and build emotional connection.

To ask someone out on a date follow one of these formats depending on what seems natural to the location/activity (yes memorize it):

"So, I'm going to go _____ on Tuesday. You should come along."

The day does not have to be Tuesday. It's the day you scheduled. You can even say, "Going to go _____ tomorrow."

Or

"So, my friends and I are going _____ tomorrow. You should come along."

Some examples:

"So, my friends and I are going skydiving on Tuesday. You should come along."

"So, I'm going to go check out the bodyworks exhibit tomorrow. You should come along."

"So, I'm going to go running in the park tomorrow. You should come along."

This phrasing takes the pressure off of it feeling like you're asking them out on a date and focuses on the fact that you're doing something fun and inviting them to join in. It's much easier for someone to say yes to join in on your fun and this will reduce the chances of them saying no to going on a date; Especially if they're not sure about you.

What you ask them to do is dependent on what they responded most favorably to in your conversations. When you've done your job being fun, interesting, displaying your uniqueness, and building an emotional connection to the point of entanglement, and you present yourself well, they will naturally want to spend more time getting to know you. They will likely say yes to coming along on your next adventure.

If they say yes, exchange numbers and tell them you'll text/call the day before you meet to confirm the details. The next chapter will talk about how to organize and plan your first date now that you have their contact information.

If they say I wish I could, but I have plans and can't make it, there are two reasons. Reason 1: They have plans. Reason 2: They're not interested in going. If they really want to spend more time with you, they will ask to go another time. Exchange numbers and work out the logistics.

If they don't want to spend more time with you, they're not interested and will say no. The reality is, not everyone will be interested, but by being fun, interesting, unique and emotionally connecting with them properly, you will have significantly increased your chances of them saying yes.

Whatever their response, it's important at this point to continue pleasing casual conversation for at least a few minutes. If you exchange numbers and then stop talking and leave it's awkward. You want to ensure the person you just asked to come join you on your next adventure feels comfortable and you do this by continuing conversation.

If they said no, continue the conversation and be fun anyway. You can always ask them to join you on one of the other five locations/activities as your discussion continues. Sometimes people say no just to test you and see your real intentions. When you keep your cool and stay fun and interesting, many times they will say "Yes" the next time you ask them to join in your future fun.

If you're Internet dating, continuation is slightly different. You'll be talking online and setting up your first date. The conversation topics and the shorter stories you created in the planning will work when talking to people online, with one adjustment: Keep e-mails and instant messages short. The more you write, the less likely they will be to respond. Keep messages to 2 or 3 sentences max and allow them to respond. If you are able to engage in flirty banter online, don't mistake the banter for emotional connection or entanglement. In my experience, it is not possible to connect emotionally via email or text or instant message. You must be interacting in person to create connection! Get to the date as soon as possible.

The following is the most successful way I ask for a first date on the Internet quickly:

Once the conversation has started and you're two or at most three messages in, ask the following:

I'm curious, which do you like better?

Mountains or ocean?
Day or night?
Coffee or tea?

When they answer, respond with your choices and then for their choice for coffee or tea tell them you know a great coffee place or tea place depending on their answer and ask them to meet. For example: You like tea? I'm more of a coffee guy but I know a great little place called Steeps Tea. Let's get together and check it out on Tuesday at 6:30 PM and see how we like each other in person."

You must give a day and time in the message; If they can't make it, they'll tell you and you can reschedule appropriately. But if you don't give a time and day they will likely not respond. This tea/coffee place is of course chosen for its proximity to the second location/activity you chose in planning so that you can go there after meeting at the coffee/tea place.

If they say they don't like coffee or tea that's ok. Say, "Interesting! I still know a great little place called Steeps Tea. They have lots of different kinds of tasty drinks. Let's get together and check it out on Tuesday at 6:30 PM and see how we like each other in person." Regardless of what they drink, they will meet you if they like you. Remember, the goal of Internet meeting is to move to a location where you can talk in person and then proceed to a second location to convey your uniqueness and have more time to create emotional entanglement.

Evaluation

Pull out a notebook, or type on your computer or however you decide to do it and answer the following questions. As before, you can download a copy of the questions with room to write at:

http://www.manipulatethedate.com

This is very important because this is how you will refine your skill and get really good at making first dates. The evaluation process allowed me to identify areas of improvement so that I was much more successful at getting first dates. If you didn't get a first date, that's ok: Be kind to yourself. You will get better as you evaluate, refine your plan, and practice. This is an experience process. The more experience you have the better you will be.

Maybe you met someone nice and made a future first date. If you are using the Internet, you've likely contacted a few people and already may have had some first dates. Maybe you have not been able to get a first date yet. Whatever your results, you're working at it. Congratulate yourself that you've gotten this far. You're doing awesome!

Thinking about your social interaction from start to finish, answer the following:

1. What conversation topics did the people you spoke with respond to

best? What conversation topics did they respond to least? Were there any topics that people you spoke with brought up that seemed engaging and you can do more research on, so you can use it in the future? Write the topics down and schedule a time to research them this week while it's fresh in your mind.

2. Of the stories that portrayed your best qualities, which one did people respond to best? Which one did they respond to least? Is there anything you can change that would increase their response to the story that did not go over as you expected? For example, can you deliver it better, memorize it better so you don't forget critical details or edit the story? If you feel there is nothing that you can change to make the bad story better, drop it and write a new one(s).

3. Did you feel the location you chose was appropriate for meeting the type of partner you want to go on a date with? If not, what are the reasons it's not appropriate? Research another location that addresses these reasons and go there next time. If you're using Internet dating websites to meet someone, you likely did not go through this phase of the meeting process and you're proceeding directly to the next chapter – The First Date.

4. Of the people you met in person, if you did exchange contact information and you're meeting for a first date in the future, think about what you talked about and write down the things you remember about them. Specifically, anything exciting or funny about your meeting, plus their favorite activities, preferences in food, eye color, clothes they were wearing, conversation topics they enjoyed, any stories they shared. Also, was there a book or something else they recommended, and anything else you can build on in future conversation?

People are always impressed when you meet them in the future and remember details about them. Remembering makes them feel special and creates emotional entanglement. It also shows you're thoughtful and pay attention to them. If you're meeting and spending time together again, it's because you see them as special and they see you as special. Remembering and talking about details from the past communicates that someone is special to you and makes you unique compared to other people they've met.

5. Were you fun and interesting and did you stay fun and interesting throughout the whole interaction process? If not, where did you stop being fun and interesting and what are the reasons? Examine those reasons and decide how to resolve them for next time.

6. If you use Internet dating to meet people, have you compared your profile to other people online? If not, compare. If you have already compared, compare again and determine if there is anything you can add or change that will separate you from the competition and make you look more unique in the eyes of the people that look at you.

7. If you are using Internet dating, reread and think about the interactions you've had so far and notice how you feel about the interactions. Were you respectful? Were the people you were interacting with respectful? If not, what can you do in the future to ensure mutual respect? Keep in mind, you can't control how other people talk to you, but you can control how you react. If something someone said or a lack of response creates an emotional reaction in you, it's your job to identify it and resolve that emotion. Are you letting the actions of strangers you've never met influence you or are you maintaining your fun and interesting attitude?

8. Think about the qualities you communicated to the people you met through your interesting conversation topics and unique stories about yourself. Are there any additional qualities you feel you want to develop that can portray you in a better way to people?

12.
Going on the First Date

You've done a great deal of work to get here. You've put effort towards your pillars of physical, mental, emotional and spiritual health and you've gone out and started meeting new people and having fun. You've already put in the time and researched the location/activity you're going to take your date on, and now it's time to focus on creating emotional entanglement with your potential partner. If you've exhausted your conversation topics from when you first met, research more (questions 11 and 12 of the planning section in the last chapter) and memorize the statement/questions you create so you're ready with them, as you need them. Also, go back and look at your qualities and write out three more stories that illustrate the qualities you wish to convey (questions 6 and 7) and memorize the stories. Also, go over the evaluation section from the last chapter and review any of the notes you made about your new potential partner making sure you memorize the details about them if you can't already remember.

When you organize the logistics of the first date, meet at the coffee shop you researched that's nearby the location/activity. When you get there, spend 30 to 45 minutes talking and getting to know each other better using your conversation generators. Also remember to bring up something you remember about them in order to connect with the fun emotions you shared on your first meeting. Letting them talk a lot shows you are a great listener, but you also need to talk and display your uniqueness and foster emotional entanglement.

If you are on a first date organized via the Internet, talk about something you noticed about them in their profile so they feel like you are paying attention. You'll also want to mention location/activity 2 that you're participating in next week. At this point, you're not going to ask them to location/activity 2, you're just going to get their opinion as you did before. For example, if a Van Gogh exhibit is in the city next week you could say, "There's a Van Gogh exhibit in town next week that I'm going to check out. What do you think about his work?" Remember, you will have to be knowledgeable about the topic you bring up as you must be able to talk about it, so remember to do some research.

If they seem uninterested in that location/activity, bring up another location/activity you researched and planned later in the conversation. Bring it up in the same fashion as you brought up the first one above. The idea is to find out which one your date would be most interested in participating in so when you ask them on the next date as outlined below, you have a much better chance of them wanting to go out with you again.

After 30 to 45 minutes at the coffee shop, go to location/activity 1 that you originally planned and enjoy getting to know each other. Focus on making sure your date is having fun and feels emotionally connected to you via the activity and your conversation. If you're concerned that you aren't emotionally connecting, relax. You did the work ahead of time in the planning phase. Trust that the location/activity is fun enough in combination with your interesting conversational skills and stories that the shared experience is emotionally bonding. Again, follow the first rule, be fun and interesting, and the rest of your planning and practice will fall into place.

As your date progresses, you're also going to be deciding if your potential partner matches the criteria you chose in the planning section of the last chapter (questions 1 through 5).

Provided you feel your potential partner meets your criteria, somewhere about three quarters of the way through the date you're going to want to go through the continuation step where you call back location/activity 2 that you mentioned you were going to next week. Remember, you should have brought this up in casual conversation at the coffee shop earlier. Now it's time to set up the next date the same way you did the first time. For example:

So, I'm going to go to that Van Gogh exhibit on Thursday. You should come along.

If you need a refresher on how to ask, go back to the Continuation step of the last chapter, review and memorize the methodology.

Again, they will say yes or no as described in the continuation section and you will adjust accordingly and then continue having fun on the current date. If you feel your potential partner does not meet your criteria, you are under no obligation to ask them out again. However, you are obligated to treat them with respect and have fun because you invited them out with you.

If they are disrespectful or abusive of you or anyone around you, you are not obligated to stay. Cut the date short. It's good to have an escape plan set in place ahead of time such as an "emergency" call from a friend where they need your help.

After the date, go through the evaluation process as follows:

1. Did you enjoy the date? What was the most enjoyable part? What would you do again if you could? If you did not enjoy the date, what were the reasons? What can you do to make the date more enjoyable next time?

2. Did your potential partner enjoy the date? What did you perceive was the most enjoyable part for them? What do you think they would do again if they could? If you think they did not enjoy the date, what were the reasons? What can you do to make the date more enjoyable next time?

3. Did your potential partner meet the criteria you desire? Are the criteria you thought you wanted in a partner accurate or does the criteria need adjusting? Adjust them accordingly if you feel they need adjusting.

Criteria are not set in stone, and as you meet people and go on dates, some people find what they desire in a partner changes. It's ok to change your mind and adjust.

4. Identify which conversation topics and stories went well and identify which did not go well. What were the reasons they went well or not well? Adjust accordingly.

5. How did it feel to go on this 2-location date? Did the two locations complement each other? If not, what should you change for next time?

13.
Date 2 and Transitioning into a Relationship

Date 2 and beyond follow the same principles as outlined before and at some point, if you're compatible, usually somewhere between date 3 and 6, you will naturally progress into a relationship.

As you progress, there are important hurdles to jump.

Kissing

There was a woman, Becky, I went out with a couple of times. On our second date we had a fun evening walking around a local hotspot and we did some people-watching. I had not kissed her on our first date because I wasn't sure she wanted to be kissed. But, on date 2, after people-watching, we went back to my place where we barbequed some steak and had dinner together. After dinner we sat on the couch and started watching a movie. I put my arm around her and we cuddled a little. After about 15 minutes I leaned in for a kiss. In the middle of our kiss she jumped up and yelled, "I can't do this!" She threw on her shoes and ran out of my house.

I called her that night but she would not pick up her phone. The next day she sent me a quick e-mail saying, "It's not you, it's me."

I tried to get some clarification, but I think she was too embarrassed by her abrupt departure to talk to me anymore.

About a month later she finally sent a message saying she really liked me, but was very nervous about kissing because she had just broken up with her past boyfriend a few days before going out with me.

There are varying opinions on when to kiss. A good guideline is either at the end of date 1 if you feel attraction for one another and the person you're with has already agreed to meet you again for date 2. If they want to spend more time with you, it's a good bet they want to kiss you but you'll have to gauge the situation. If they're lingering at the end of your date, they're most likely waiting and wanting to be kissed. If they haven't agreed to another date, it's an indication that the date isn't going well and a kiss attempt may be unwelcome.

The kiss I have found most successful (whether you're a man or woman) is to take a slow step into their personal space and notice their reaction. You should already be close to each other as part of natural conversation before you take a step or lean in. If they lean forward towards you, go in for the kiss. If they step, lean, or jump back, then you step back and don't go for the kiss.

It's important that if you're unsuccessful in having a kiss at first, both of you could feel uncomfortable moving forward. You must take the pressure off of the situation by starting another conversation topic.

They didn't kiss you for a few reasons. Either because they're not interested, or because they are not emotionally connected enough with you yet to feel comfortable kissing yet. It could be they don't kiss anyone until the 3rd date. You really don't know. Focus on continuing to be fun and interesting. It's ok to try again on the next date provided things are going well.

If you're worried about the kiss, remember, it can't be much worse than someone jumping up and running out of your house.

Texting

Texting – let's lump instant messaging, e-mail and social networking into this category as well. These are excellent written tools to save time and maintain friendships and relationships.

When it comes to dating, there is a sequence that should be followed to ensure success.

To set up a first date, whether you've met in person or online, avoid as much electronic communication as possible. Use texting as a means to sort out the logistics of a date. Why? Simply put, you cannot emotionally connect via text. You may have excellent conversation, be flirty, and banter well, but this does not translate into emotional entanglement. You can only create emotional involvement by talking in person or in some cases on the telephone. This is because you can't see or hear how each of you responds physically to what is being said. Key information you need to determine if you're emotionally connecting with someone is missing when you can't see or hear them. Without the whole picture, you're relying on a small part of the full communication process.

On my dates, every single person I have ever met has said meeting and seeing someone in person is very different than talking via text. A person's personality cannot be conveyed or interpreted the same way as it is when meeting face to face. As such, in the beginning, only use texting as an organizational tool for dating.

As you progress in a relationship, texting (and any written communication) can be an excellent tool to maintain your relationship by saying nice things to your partner and letting them know you're thinking about them and how special they are to you (as long as you don't overdo it).

Texting is a terrible tool to rely on in an argument. Never start and fight via text. Check yourself and examine what you write. If what you say is negative in any way, do not send the message. Instead, stop writing immediately, call or meet your partner in person and have a real conversation. The same goes for receiving a nasty text/e-mail. When it comes to relationships and dating, do not respond in writing to anything that is insulting or starts a fight.

Text arguments spiral out of control quickly because neither of you can see or hear the hurt and other emotions you are causing each other via written communication.

Who Should Pay?

This can be a hotly debated topic and great to talk about with your potential partner – on the 3rd date and not before unless they bring it up.

Generally, the person who did the inviting to the first date should be paying for the first date. Now, if you remember, I've been on thousands of dates and that got expensive fast! I learned quickly to set up first dates that were fun, interesting, and free! I recommend the same.

Don't spend your money trying to buy someone's affection. Instead, get to know them and build emotional entanglement first. If they are a good match, you'll go on a second date.

On a second date, I, as the asker, would pay at the first half of the 2 location second date with the agreement that at the second location, they would pay. I also ensured the costs at either location were not extremely different. For example, if we met for coffee followed by a walk in the park, I usually pay for the coffee and say, "I'll get the coffees and you get the bottles of water we need for our walk."

Then on the 3rd date I would bring up paying in casual conversation by saying this:

My friend Sally just went on a first date with a guy she's been friends with for about five years. They were both in relationships with other people and newly single and he asked her out. They went for dinner and she insisted they split the cheque. I think, since it was their first date and he asked her out, he should have picked up the bill and she could have paid on the next date. What do you think?

This opens up the topic nicely on the third date after you've already had a second date where both of you paid for a portion to establish equality.

Age

Age is an interesting topic that is important to some and irrelevant to others.

In online dating, men in general want to date women that are younger. Women in general have a narrow age range where they want to date someone that is about five to eight years of their own age.

Outside the Internet, in the real world, people's age ranges tend to be broader and age gaps can vary geographically and culturally. It's been my experience that the age gap between two people is proportional to a combination of the following factors:

1. Looks and physical fitness.
2. Financial fitness.
3. Social fitness and status.
4. Emotional entanglement.

Age can be a factor in dating, but it can take a back seat to those four factors.

My friend Betty, who was 22 at the time, was walking down the street and a man who she thought must have been about 50 started flirting with her at a corner coffee shop. Although she thought his flirting was cute at first, it quickly became uncomfortable because he clearly wanted to take her out on a date and she had to decline. She told me she felt uncomfortable because he was older than her dad and she felt the age difference was too great.

So I asked her, "What did he look like?"

She said, "He was a bit overweight with grey hair."

I said, "Ok, so he was about 50. I know you like Brad Pitt. He's about 50. If he looked like Brad Pitt, would you have gone out with him?"

She said, "Oh my God! For sure!"

So it wasn't the age difference. In Betty's case it was looks, money and celebrity status.

Provided both are legal adults, the only two people that an age difference should concern, is you and the person you're in a relationship with.

Being Intimate

Awhile back I had some severe testicle pain. I went to the doctor to see what was wrong.

At one point, the doctor asked if I felt any lumps on my testicle and I said, "I think there might be a small one, but I'm not sure."

My doctor said, "Ok. Show me where."

So I'm lying on my back, fully exposed, trying to feel where the lump is to show him and I can't find it because the testicle has a mind of its own and keeps popping out of my hand as I apply pressure to find the lump.

The nurse says, "Here let me hold it for you." And she gets a firm yet gentle grip on my testicle.

At this point, I have both hands free to find the lump and as I'm feeling around, I look down and see the doctors face a few inches from my crotch, the nurse is holding my testicle, and she says, "Wow, he's in really great shape!"

And he says, "Yes he is!"

I had to bite my tongue to keep from laughing hysterically as their faces stared at my naked crotch, my testicles in the nurse's hands.

And then I said it: "You know… this isn't the threesome I was looking for!"

Talk about awkward! Turns out everything was ok with my health. They couldn't find anything and sent me for more tests and an ultrasound and it showed a small hernia that was radiating pain.

Like my nonsexual threesome in the doctor's office, for some people, sex is an awkward situation. There is so much literature out there with varying opinions on when to have it, if you should have it, how to have it etc.

In Manipulate the Date rule number 4 is "Consent both verbal and physical." Talk about sex in conversation before you have it. Make sure you're both on the same page about safety, consent, and comfort. If one of you is not comfortable, then you're both not ready to have sex. Build emotional entanglement so you're connected and ready to share a wonderful experience.

If you're not sure how to bring the conversation of sex up, here are some indirect conversation starters you can use on a first date and have a comfortable and interesting conversation.

My friend's parents just got divorced recently and I'm curious what it's going to be like for them to start dating? I mean, they've been married for so long I wonder how they're going to feel dating and eventually having sex with someone new for the first time? What do you think that would be like?

Or:

I was reading an article the other day about how teenagers that take a vow of abstinence before marriage have support groups for each other to help them get through their sexual urges. What do you think about that?

As these conversation topics progress, you will be able to talk about sex in a constructive way.

If you're not sure if you're ready to have sex yet, here are some questions to ask yourself to help you evaluate.

1. Do I really like this person? Do I feel there is emotional entanglement?

2. What personal beliefs do I have about sex? What religious beliefs do I have about sex? How are these beliefs affecting my decision? Does my potential partner share my beliefs?

3. Do I feel pressured by this person or are they ensuring I feel safe and comfortable?

4. Are there any lingering feelings and memories I have towards someone else in a previous relationship that are affecting me? How are these feelings and memories affecting me? How can I help resolve these feelings so I can enjoy my current experience?

5. Are there any past traumatic experiences that I've experienced that are affecting me? This can be very difficult.

I once had a relationship with a woman who was raped when she was younger and many times she was very nervous when we became intimate. We both had to take extra steps to ensure she felt safe and comfortable and many times, if she were experiencing painful emotions we would talk and I would hold her in my arms until she felt better.

6. Are alcohol and/or drugs affecting my decisions?

I had a first date with a woman, Janice. I picked her up at her place and took her to Boston Pizza for a quick coffee – we met online and had instant chemistry and after talking for five minutes decided to move things along quickly and I picked her up at her place an hour later.

We went into the lounge and the waitress told us the 32 oz. schooners were on special. Janice said she'd love one, so we ordered a couple. Janice was also hungry, so she ordered food and started drinking her schooner.

After about 4 of the 32 oz., Janice passed out. I wasn't sure what was happening but the food came. I had it packed up, paid the cheque and carried her back to my van (which at the time was white with no windows – yes, I know; was as bad as that sounds). The waitress did not look impressed with me and I'm sure it looked like I was some sort of pervert who had drugged my date.

I drove her home and as I'm pulling into to her place she wakes up and is a bit groggy. She realizes that she passed out and I asked her, "Are you ok? Has this happened to you before?"

She said, "No, I don't normally drink and I'm on some medication that makes me sleepy. I guess I shouldn't have mixed the two. I'm sorry."

I said, "It's ok," and walked her to the door – mostly because it was minus 25 out and I wanted to make sure she didn't pass out again and freeze before she got inside.

She searched in her little purse (about the size of a man's wallet) for her keys for a minute… then two minutes… then three minutes and we're freezing!

I said, "Do you want me to help with your key?"

She said, "Yes!" and handed me her purse.

I peered inside and all that was there was a compact mirror and a tube of lipstick. No ID, no money, no keys, no nothing. She had clearly decided she was going to order food and drinks intending for me to pay for everything. I felt used and taken advantage of.

I said, "There's no key in here."

So she rang the doorbell (she lived in her brother's basement suite) for someone to let her in. It was 11 p.m. on a Tuesday night and her brother's family was unimpressed with us ringing the doorbell.

Her sister-in-law came to the door and screamed at us both about how irresponsible we were and how we'd woken up the kids and the whole household. I stood there shocked. It was like looking at a train wreck. I didn't want to be there but I couldn't help but watch, dumbfounded in silence. Janice's sister-in-law finished yelling, opened the basement suite door and stormed off.

I said, "Well Janice, it was a pleasure meeting you." And I turned around to leave.

She grabbed my arm and said, "Hey, please wait. Come inside for a minute. I don't want you to leave on this crazy note. Come inside and have some tea."

I said, "Ok." And followed her down the steps into her apartment.

What I saw, I will always remember. She had three cats, two hamsters, and floating through the air was fur and dander. I grew up with animals so I'm a little familiar with how much they shed, and I'm guessing there was enough fur on the furniture and floating in the air that she had not cleaned her place in two years. I have a slight allergy to cats – I can be around them, I can pet them, and after a couple hours I get a little itchy. But, as soon I was inside Janice's place, my throat started to constrict and my eyes were watering from the cat hair in the air.

As soon as we're inside, Janice said, "I have to go to the bathroom. I'll be right back. Sit down on the couch."

I sat down and my clothes were immediately covered in cat hair. To finish me off, her cats came over and started rubbing all over my legs – what is it about cats that they seem to know when you're allergic and they instinctually rub themselves all over you?

After a few minutes Janice came out of the bathroom wearing lingerie. She sat down beside me and leaned in for a kiss.

At this point, I was thoroughly disgusted. She'd already passed out on me.

I had to carry her out of the restaurant, which made me look like some sort of predator. She clearly expected me to be a sugar daddy and pay for her food and drinks. Her sister- in-law just tore me a new "A" and I was having trouble breathing because her apartment was so filthy dirty!

Covered in cat hair, I got up, said "No thank you!" and I got the hell out of there!

Sometimes people get into sexual situations prematurely because drugs and/or alcohol compromise their decision-making process just like Janice. Sometimes it doesn't take much. Ensure you are sober before making these kinds of decisions. In fact, when you're Manipulating the Date be sober period!

Some people think it's easier to meet potential partners while drinking. Being sober allows you to be a better conversationalist and allows you to portray uniqueness and work on emotionally entangling with potential partners. It allows you to listen to the person you're talking to and gauge how to respond in a way that is appropriate.

Being sober will result in better dates and allow you to make clear headed decisions, especially when it comes to becoming intimate at a time that is right for both of you.

As you've seen so far, there are many moving parts in the Manipulate the Date process and being sober and able to think on your feet is required to make sure you're allowing yourself to be as successful as possible with a new potential partner.

Intimacy Challenges

Sometimes, once you've had sex, for one reason or another, there's a distinct lack of fireworks in the bedroom. You run hot when your partner runs cold, wires get crossed, signals get mixed, people get bored or tired... the list can go on and on, and the problem can seem bigger and bigger, unless you do something about it.

But where do you start?

Great sex doesn't just happen by snapping your fingers. Here's some advice I've given clients that has helped them work through relationship issues and have better sex.

1. Stop focusing on sex: The problem might not be physical, but rather a lack of emotional connection. Engage in activities that focus on building up your emotional bonds. Usually, the stronger the emotional entanglement, the better the sex.

2. Do something wild and/or scary together: Ride a rollercoaster with your partner, go skydiving or bungee jumping. The excitement and the adrenaline rush will get you hotter for each other. When you're both sharing an experience that is exhilarating and causes you fear, you can bond on an emotional level and that in turn can be channeled into better, exciting sex. If you're not up for jumping out of a plane, just snuggle up on the couch and watch a scary movie.

3. Recognize that sex is not a sprint, but a marathon: When you're single you may have the challenge of going a long time without sex, whether you want to or not. If it's been awhile and you finally get to it with a new partner, it's sometimes over as fast as it began. Take your time and make it last. Work at going at a slower pace and savor the experience.

4. Utilize technology: Send your partner a sexy text/email while they're at work. Engage in sexting only if you've established trust with your partner. In today's world of texting, picking up the phone and calling to connect can create more intimacy as well.

5. Sometimes, forget about technology: Social media and smartphones have made it more difficult for people to connect on an emotional level. Write a good old-fashioned letter with pen and paper to your partner. Tell them how much they mean to you, how attractive they are, and describe what excites you about them and why.

6. Get creative with the location: Sex isn't just for the bedroom. Find other places in your house/apartment to have sex; do it in the car or a backyard, role-play, experiment with sex toys and new positions. Make it fun and exciting.

7. Focus on foreplay: There's a reason to engage in foreplay – it stimulates both partners' sexuality, lowers inhibitions, and increases emotional intimacy.

8. Take a deep breath and relax: Being relaxed leads to a stronger erection for men and increased sensations for women. Never put expectations on sex, just go with the flow and let it happen. Massage and tickle each other leading up to sex to lighten the mood.

9. Share what you really want: Be honest and tell each other what you like, what works and what doesn't, new positions or techniques you want to try. This level of sexual awareness will take your emotional and sexual relationships to new heights.

10. Focus on what you like about your partner: Some people focus on what they dislike about their partner and feelings of resentment accumulate and emotional connection fades.

11. Take care of the other stuff: While sex is always great at the beginning of any relationship, factors like stress, money, work and children start taking priority in people's lives. Manage your life effectively so you can enjoy being with another person.

12. Picture yourself having sex: Spend five to 10 minutes a day picturing yourself having great sex with your partner. Think about the sounds, sights, smells and how you feel during sex. Many people focus on the physical aspects of sex and ignore the fact that sex can be a mentally and emotionally stimulating experience. The more you prepare mentally, the more amazing the physical becomes.

13. Clear your head: If you're thinking about going to work or paying the bills during sex, you're not having good sex. Clear your head before you get to bed: de-stress from your work and hectic personal life and use this time to focus on your partner.

14. Vary the time of day you have sex: For example, if you have sex at night, try morning sex and vice-versa. On weekends, have sex in the afternoon, before or after lunch or before you go out at night.

15. Change Up Your Look: Women – Try a new hair color or guys a new type of facial hair. When you feel like a new person, sex becomes more exciting for you and your partner.

16. Put on something your partner will be excited by: Maybe it's a little black dress or a something simple like a white tee. Whatever it is, putting on something that excites your partner will make things a lot more thrilling. And if you do notice your partner wearing something you like, compliment them!

17. Touch the right spots: Have your partner lie down on his or her stomach naked. Start massaging from the feet and work up to his or her

head. "A relaxed body allows for better blood flow to the extremities which can lead to a stronger erection for men and increased sensations for women," Throw in a little dirty talk and/or massage oil.

18. Communication: The secret to any long-lasting relationship is being comfortable talking about the good and bad. If sex is the issue, make sure your partner knows.

The other challenge you may face is, if you, or the person you're dating (or both of you) are a virgin(s). Pressure can come from everywhere when someone has not yet had sex. There are many reasons not to have had sex: Maybe your cultural or religious beliefs are focused on sex and marriage. Maybe you've not had or met the right person in your life to have sex for the first time. Pressure from society, religion, culture, friends, social anxiety issues, and even from your partner can be overwhelming.

Do your best to let go of the influence of others and maintain your beliefs and what makes you feel comfortable. You will have to talk to your partner about your feelings about your virginity or theirs and what each of your expectations are. If you've never had sex before, it's a big first step and you should be able to do it openly and freely with the person of your choosing.

The greater your emotional entanglement with someone, the better the experience will be for both of you. Focus on making sure you feel safe and comfortable while honoring each of your beliefs. If you're potential partner is unable to support your beliefs, then you will have to decide where to go from there.

Getting Over Rejection

Being as socially awkward as I was when I was younger, and then participating in Internet dating, has definitely made me an expert on rejection... Literally... I have been rejected thousands of times.

A few years back, I went on an Internet date with Nora. It was 2 weeks before Christmas. The date went well; however, with it being close to Christmas our schedules made it difficult to connect in person. We stuck to talking on the phone and text messages to keep in contact.

On Christmas Eve I was visiting with my mom and Nora had plans to play pool and visit with friends at a local watering hole. We texted on and off throughout the night, and she told me how much fun she was having. I was finished visiting with my family at about 10 PM and I asked to come join her.

She said it would be awkward if I showed up and she wasn't ready to introduce me to her friends after only 2 weeks. I stayed home and we continued to text as her festivities progressed. She filled me in on tidbits of the night's activities and even talked about a cool guy her friend brought along who was visiting from Australia for 2 weeks and seemed to be the life of the party.

Because of planned vacations on both our parts, our schedules finally caught up with each other towards mid-January. We had a couple more dates and the end of January came and she texted she couldn't see me anymore with no explanation.

Our dates and conversation went well and it did not make sense to me that she suddenly went cold turkey, so I pressed the issue and asked, "What's changed?"

She confessed, "I'm pregnant."

I said, "Ummm, ok, who's the father?"

She said, "Remember that guy visiting from Australia on Christmas Eve?"

I said, "Yeah."

She said, "Well I slept with him because he was fun and I was feeling lonely that night and now I'm pregnant. It's crazy because he's in Australia and wants nothing to do with me or the baby, but I'm going to keep it anyway."

While I was floored by the situation, I was actually very thankful that she was honest with me. We had not been physically intimate to that point, however, should she have been less honest, she could have slept with me and claimed the baby was mine.

It was a singularly unique experience for me. I was not angry. We had only known each other for 2 weeks when she had her one-night-stand and there was no commitment on either of our parts. We had not talked about being in a monogamous relationship because we hadn't built enough emotional entanglement. At the same time, I was disappointed and I felt rejected.

I thought about it and realized the reason I felt rejected was because instead of spending time with me on Christmas, Nora told me to stay home and picked up a random stranger. I also really liked her and saw a potential future together that was curtailed by some random man from another country she never saw again. That's a tough pill to swallow when she told me I was a great guy yet she still felt a stranger was who she needed that night.

I realized then that Nora's rejection of someone she deemed a "great guy" (as she described me) was not about me. Certainly, the rejection felt like it was about me, because ultimately I'm the one that was rejected, but her rejection was really a reflection of her wants and desires and had nothing to do with me as a person.

Applying that thought to all the other times I was rejected allowed me to realize being rejected early on was a blessing because it gave me the freedom to pursue someone who is a better match instead of committing my precious time, effort, and emotional stability to someone whose desires I could never fulfill.

There are two types of rejection:

The first is long-term relationship rejection where you'll have to get over the end of your relationship. Recovering from this type of rejection is covered earlier in the "getting over the end of a relationship" section in Chapter 5 Manipulation of Self – The 4 Pillars.

The second is short-term dating rejection. This type of rejection can occur at any stage of dating from before you've even met someone (like Internet dating where you can send 50 messages and no one responds leading to feelings of rejection), to being stood up, to going on a few dates and a relationship not progressing, to becoming emotionally entangled with someone.

When dealing with this kind of rejection it's very easy to get bitter and jaded. Of all my hypnotherapy clients, friends, and myself that have dated, or are dating, we have all experienced this rejection at some point. Unsuccessful dating can be extremely frustrating!

In these cases, it's important to have friends that you can talk to that will cheer you up. When you're rejected, you can fall into the "dating sucks" or "no one wants to date me" mode, which reinforces itself. This can be very depressing. This is when you have to remember that your time, effort and emotional stability are more important than someone you barely know.

The best way to recover from short term dating rejection is to get out and meet someone new. When you're in rejection mode, meeting someone new that is genuinely interested erases and/or overpowers feelings of short term dating rejection within seconds. The excitement of meeting someone new is infectious and overpowers your negative emotions. You immediately forget there was someone that just rejected you. Yes, it's cliché: "When you fall, get back up on that horse!"

If you find meeting someone new does not alleviate these negative feelings, it can be a sign of deeper issues that you may wish to resolve. If you find this is the case, review the chapters covering the pillars of physical, mental, emotional and spiritual health, decide on an action plan, and improve your thoughts and outlook.

Whether you're being rejected (or you are rejecting someone I.E. deciding there is no basis to further your relationship), there are rules you should follow:

1. Be respectful:
Respect that the other person is a human being with emotions and treat them well and be kind. Just because your connection did not work out now does not mean you'll never see them again. I have gone on many dates where women did not have romantic interest and after a time, we became friends. Yes, it stings emotionally when feelings are not reciprocated, however, once you move on and date someone new, that sting resolves itself and you have an opportunity to create another kind of relationship provided you've been mutually respectful.

2. Be honest:
Lying to spare someone's feelings does not help you or them in the long run. It compounds hurt feelings. You can be diplomatic if need be, but always be honest.

3. Be responsible for yourself:
You are only responsible for your own feelings and wellbeing. You can't

change how someone else feels and you are not responsible for how they react. You are responsible for what you say and what you do. Be calm and be graceful no matter the other's reactions.

4. Be mature:
Don't air your hurt feelings on social media. Posting angry comments is a reflection of your emotional state and portrays you as emotionally immature. It's great to talk to friends in person or by telephone and seek support. Social media responses to angry relationship posts are not support even if they seem supportive. They play into your desire to find negative attention and validation, and will only prolong your pain. When you meet someone new and they look at your social media, ask yourself if they would really want to begin a relationship with you if you're airing hurt feelings about other people publicly. Emotionally stable and mature adults, who want to be in a healthy relationship, look for stability and maturity in their partners.

Deciding You're in a Relationship

How do you know when it's time to be in a relationship? Turns out, that's a question with a lot of answers. To find out, I've asked the following question on many first dates as a conversation topic:

My friend Trina says after six dates with a man, she knows for sure whether she wants to pursue a romantic relationship. Do you think six dates is enough? Or should it be less? Or should it be more?

The common answer is: "It depends"

Based on the answers I've received; the consensus seems to be between three to eight dates. The number also depends on your individual and shared experiences.

Whatever the number is, there is a bigger picture to focus on: You and your potential partner should spend enough time together and know each other well enough so you're both comfortable to talk about the subject.

Some people decide to have a relationship talk before sex, some people after. It's hard to predict when to have the talk to decide you're in a relationship, but one thing is certain: You must have the talk and both of you must decide that you are in a relationship for things to progress.

If you don't have the talk, the dating process you've gone through so far can quickly fall apart. This is because emotional entanglement has occurred and is still developing. To ensure your entanglement remains intact, trust must be established. Without trust, doubt will creep into your new partner's mind and into yours as well. Doubt creates conflict. Honesty and trust strengthens and resolves. Create a trusting and honest relationship.

One common issue I've seen meeting with women on the Internet is they can have an over-inflated sense of self-worth. This goes for men too. They claim they're "worth it." That's great except they don't back it up. It's not enough to say you're worth it, and it's not enough to be worth it while taking no action to prove it. You must demonstrate to your partner that you are worth it continually over the course of dating, and over the course of your relationship. As you continue to demonstrate your uniqueness and value you continue to strengthen the relationship. The same goes for your partner.

In fact, as you demonstrate your uniqueness and value, if your partner does not contribute to the relationship by demonstrating uniqueness and value consistently, this can become a source of hard feelings and negative emotion. This negative emotion sabotages emotional entanglement and the relationship can fall apart.

Demonstrating uniqueness and value can take many forms whether you're male or female. These values may be physical, emotional, mental, spiritual, and/or financial. This value is based on what your partner perceives to be important (not what you perceive is valuable).

You have to feel wanted and make your partner feel wanted. For example, take the lyrics from Beyoncé's song "Single Ladies." The chorus line says, "If you like it, then you should have put a ring on it!" That's a very one-sided stance of a relationship, especially when relationships are two-way streets. If you want the ring, what are you doing to make your partner feel wanted? You must continuously engage each other's emotions to make your bond stronger.

Afterword

I hope you have exciting dates with amazing people and I hope this process helps you create the relationship of your dreams! When the relationship you've been working for emerges, savor it! Love it! Enjoy it with all your heart and soul.

When that special partner is part of your life, please remember to keep the dating process alive with each other. Your relationship started because you manipulated the dates with your partner to be fun, interesting, unique and emotionally entangling. This is what brought you together in the first place and made your relationship successful.

To maintain that success, keep dating your partner with the same vigor you began your relationship with! Set aside a time at least once a week and have a date together where you have researched and planned a new location/activity. These new experiences will continue to foster your unique bond and further strengthen your emotional entanglement.

Don't fall into the habit of routine where you become complacent and stop dating each other. It's easy to do. It's one of the primary reasons my relationships failed in the past. It's one of the primary relationship issues my clients have… But that's another book for another time!

Thank you for reading.

I wish you great dating and relationship success!

Colin Christopher
Edmonton, Alberta Canada,
December 12, 2015

Learning Resources

Colin's TV Interviews and featured articles:
http://www.colinontv.com/

Success Through Manipulation Book:
http://www.successthroughmanipulationbook.com/

Free Weight Loss Program Using Hypnosis:
http://www.freeloseweighthypnosis.com/

Always Afraid? Conquer Your Fear Using Hypnosis:
http://www.alwaysafraid.com/

Hypnosis for Child Birth:
http://www.easybabybirth.com/

Hypnosis Health Store:
http://www.hypnosishealthstore.com/

Free Hypnotist Course:
http://www.freehypnotistcourse.com/

Colin Christopher's Official Hypnosis Site:
http://www.colinchristopher.com/

Colin Christopher's Success Through Manipulation Speaking Site:
http://www.successthroughmanipulation.com/

Facebook:
http://www.facebook.com/colinchristopher/

Twitter:
http://www.twitter.com/colinontv/

LinkedIn:
http://www.linkedin.com/in/colinchristopher/

COLIN CHRISTOPHER
www.colinontv.com

AS FEATURED ON

Phone: 780-903-1677
Email: info@colinchristopher.com

LOSE WEIGHT WITH HYPNOSIS FOR FREE

In the news today, they say obesity is an epidemic. If this is true for you and you want to lose weight, there is help. And it's FREE.

When it comes to weight, lighter people think differently than heavier people. Because they think differently, lighter people don't have the mental barriers that heavier people do.

Using this FREE hypnosis program, you're going to put your mind and body into a relaxed state. Then you're going to train your subconscious mind to think like lighter people do. That way you can break through the mental barriers that are keeping you heavy!

www.freeloseweighthypnosis.com

ALWAYS AFRAID?
CONQUER YOUR FEAR!

Does Fear hold you back? Do you have anxiety?
Phobia's get you down?

Stage Fright?   Bees?
Snakes?   Anxiety?
Spiders?   Phobia?

What are you afraid of?

There is help. You're not alone.

Ever wonder why you're afraid of something and someone else isn't? It's because they react differently than you do. Change how you react so you are comfortable and calm.

Using this hypnosis program, you're going to put your mind and body into a relaxed state to train your subconscious mind and change your fight or flight response. That way you can break through the mental barriers that make you afraid!

Try it. It's safe. It's relaxing. You have nothing to fear but fear itself!

www.alwaysafraid.com

EASY BABY BIRTH
HYPNOSIS TO HELP PREGNANCY AND DELIVERY

Hypnosis for childbirth is becoming more and more popular with celebrities like Jessica Alba, Kim Kardashian and Princess Kate Middleton using hypnosis to help with their pregnancies.

Expecting moms everywhere are wondering if hypnosis is right for them. The simple answer is yes! Hypnosis can have a dramatic effect throughout all stages of pregnancy, helping women cope with everything from morning sickness, to stress, to pain and delivery.

Try the first module for free and see how relaxed you'll feel at:
www.easybabybirth.com

LEARN HOW TO BECOME A STAGE HYPNOTIST FOR FREE!

Love hypnosis or just curious how it works?

Colin Christopher has been in front of over 250,000 people all over the world and has performed for cruise lines, resorts, casinos, corporations, and more. He is a stage hypnosis instructor certified by The American Council of Hypnotist Examiners and a practicing clinical hypnotherapist who will show you what it takes to be a successful hypnotist.

In this FREE online course you will learn:

What it takes to get started in the business
How to run successful shows and seminars from start to finish
What hypnosis is and how it works
Why you should learn hypnotherapy
What can go right and what can go wrong in your shows
How to write successful hypnosis scripts
The ins and outs of creating self help products
How to market yourself to cruise ships, resorts, casinos, corporations, or any other client you want

…and much, much more!

Sign up today! It's FREE.

www.freehypnotistcourse.com

GET SOCIAL AND STAY INFORMED

Facebook:

www.facebook.com/colinchristopher/

Twitter:

www.twitter.com/colinontv/

LinkedIn:

www.linkedin.com/in/colinchristopher/

About the Author

Colin Christopher is a keynote speaker, stage hypnotist and sought after authority in hypnosis appearing all over the world on networks like ABC, CBS, NBC, FOX, ESPN, Global, City, CTV and many others.

As a clinical hypnotherapist, hypnosis instructor, and author, Colin has also been featured in hundreds of prominent publications like the LA Times, Daily Mail UK, Metro New York, Psychology Today and ELLE.

Visit http://www.colinontv.com and watch TV interviews and read many of his feature articles.

Made in the USA
Charleston, SC
12 January 2016